Sacred Self

A Journey to Embracing Feminine Wholeness

Through Nurturing the Body, Mind, and Soul

By

Malia Grace

Contents

Introduction 6

Introduction to caring for your Sacred Self.... 20

    The Importance of Self-Care for Women 23

    The Connection Between Feminine Energy and Wellness 31

    Our Approach to caring for your Sacred Self 35

Embracing Feminine Energy 38

    Understanding Feminine Energy 40

    The Importance of a Healthy Feminine Energy 44

    Balancing Masculine and Feminine Energies 45

    How Are Masculine and Feminine Energies Interconnected? 46

    Activating Your Feminine Power 52

    Your Relationship with the Seasons and Elements 54

Nourishing Your Body 65

    Establishing a Clean Eating Lifestyle 67

    Balancing Hormones Through Nutrition 86

Detoxifying Your Environment 93

    The Importance of Clean Products 95

    Choosing Clean Beauty Products 97

    Safe Lotions, Deodorants, Vaginal Lubricants and Sunscreens .100

    Choosing Natural Household Cleaners 108

    Creating a Toxin-Free Home 109

Movement and Exercise 117

    The Benefits of Regular Movement 118

Yoga for Women's Wellness 130

The Power of Yoga..130

Developing a Personal Yoga Practice............................135

Breathing Techniques...138

Meditation and Mindfulness 142

The Benefits of Meditation...............................144

Techniques for Mindfulness Meditation....................145

Cultivating a Daily Meditation Practice 148

Creating a Sanctuary in Your Home............ 151

The Importance of Sacred Space...........................152

Designing Your Sanctuary................................157

Infusing Your Sanctuary with Positive Energy 158

Crystals for Healing and Chakra Balance 162

An Introduction to Crystal Healing 163

Crystals for Balancing Chakras..........................166

How to Unblock a Chakra 168

Incorporating Crystals Into Daily Life..................172

Self-Care Rituals for Women.................... 176

The Importance of Self-Care.............................178

Establishing a Self-Care Routine........................180

Self-Care Practices for Mind, Body, and Spirit 183

Cultivating Positive Relationships............. 192

The Importance of Supportive Relationships 193

Establishing Boundaries and Communicating Needs........199

Building a Community of Empowerment....................207

Integrating Spirituality and Personal Growth 211

Exploring Your Spiritual Path............................214

Aligning Your Life with Your Values 223

The Power of Gratitude and Affirmations 227

Developing a Gratitude Practice....................................230

Embracing Your Wholeness.........................240

Reflecting on Your Journey...241

Maintaining Balance and Harmony 242

Continuing Your Path to Healing....................................244

Conclusion 247

Acknowledgments 255

Introduction

This is my why.

I decided to create this book out of a desire to empower women to unlock their inner strength, embrace their feminine power, and savor every moment of their unique journey on this earth. My intention is to help women realize they have the power to heal themselves. Through self-care and self-love, balancing nutrition, detoxification, movement, mindfulness, and spirituality we can improve our health and inner strength so we can enjoy our life in the body we're given, listen to our soul's calling, and show up in this world expressing our feminine power with love, grace, and joy! For doing so is truly sacred.

You may wonder, why would my self-care be sacred and what does it mean for something to be sacred? In this context, the sacred is something that is treated with great respect and dignity. It commands a sense of awe and inspires a feeling of reverence in those who encounter it. Self-care is considered sacred in many cultures because it aligns with deeper philosophical and spiritual principles that emphasize the holistic well-being of individuals. Ultimately, it's deeply rooted in the belief that caring for oneself is not only a personal responsibility but also a sacred duty that contributes to the greater harmony of the individual and the community. I hope that after reading this book you'll view self-care and self-love as a sacred act and gift you can give to yourself.

I'm not just an author but a woman who has personally walked the path I am guiding you on. I have devoted the last 20 years of my life to understanding and applying the principles of healthy living. However, my journey was not always smooth. Like you, I too have struggled with the pressures and demands of modern life.

Although my journey has not been easy, it's mine and I know that the heartache I've endured and the mistakes I've made have led me to where I am today. I have learned lessons from my mistakes, even though some of them I've made repeatedly. I'm learning to be patient with myself, accept my flaws as they are, and remember to love myself despite them.

When I look back, I realize that I was being called to elevate myself when I experienced deep emotional, heart-wrenching pain that I now see as catalysts meant to shove me onto the path I was meant to walk. Because I ignored the whispers of my inner knowing, it took big explosions to wake me up to a new level of consciousness. Divorce in my early 30s forced me to really look at my past, my patterns, and my worth. My dad dying of lung cancer when I was in my 40s pushed me to understand what truly causes illness and led me on a path to invest in WELLness instead of ILLness. I found myself depleted, heartbroken over the loss of my dad, and experienced severe fatigue, joint pain, and anger in my heart for many years prior to his passing. Reading The Truth About Cancer and learning about the healing power of plants and essential oils pushed me to pay attention to what I can do to minimize my personal exposure to toxins.

Prior to the death of my dad, however, I remember days of relentless working, rarely pausing to rest or rejuvenate, and suppressing my feelings. The result was a health and emotional breakdown that left me depleted in more ways than one. This was my wake-up call, the impetus that propelled me into the world of holistic wellness. I dove into researching and studying various facets of healthy living—from nutrition, essential oils, and detoxification to more recently meditation, movement, mindfulness, and beyond. As I write this, the past year was the third big bang that catapulted me to really think about what my purpose is, figure out what I really want in life and led me to connect with something greater than myself through meditation, journaling, and mindfulness.

I'm thankful for these lessons because they have led me to where I am today. The lessons have been hard however! Really hard! I nearly blew up my current marriage and found myself numb, holding a lifetime worth of anger and resentment in my soul that was crushing me. My hips ached so badly I could barely stand at times and see now that I was merely going through the motions in life. I realized that for so long I silenced my voice to keep the peace, and brick by brick put up walls around myself to the point I nearly trapped myself in without even a roof or window to escape out of.

Over my lifetime, I have come to recognize that old familial patterns have not served me well and that I can break those patterns and change them for the better. During my personal transformation, I found it important to show myself love and compassion as well as surround myself with people who believed in me, especially when I found it difficult to believe in myself.

I've also seen firsthand the transformative power of holistic health practices. From regaining my vitality through clean eating and regular movement to incorporating self-care practices, I found peace and balance by integrating mindfulness, journaling, and meditation into my daily routine. I've experienced the profound impact of embracing a holistic approach to wellness.

I have also learned that the body keeps score. If we bottle-up emotions, they tend to show up in the body as discomfort and pain whether we like it or not. However, processing those suppressed feelings can and will set you free.

Throughout my journey, I've also found that the key to embracing wholeness extends beyond diet and exercise; it's about nurturing your physical body and your emotional, mental, and spiritual well-being. It's about creating harmony in all aspects of your life. This understanding led me to curate a comprehensive approach to wellness that embraces the totality of existence encapsulated in this book.

If you are a woman who has experienced trauma or painful loss, if you're having health problems or just finding that you're out of balance and can use some guidance, this book is for you. It's time to release, heal, grow, and become the woman—the goddess—you are meant to be.

Many women have gone through life-altering events that left them devastated, lost, ill, off-balance, and disconnected from their true selves. It's okay if you've forgotten who you are. Welcome back to a new and improved you!

Life is about change, so embrace it! Change is one of the few constants in this world. Whether change is positive or negative, it comes with lessons that enrich your life experience and cultivate resilience. They teach you to adapt, persevere, and overcome. Change is scary, I know, but it's also a very powerful motivator. Trying to resist inevitable change and control anything other than our own emotions and actions can lead to disconnection and disappointment. I have found that the more rigid we are, the more likely we are to crack. So, embrace the changes in you; change is growth and that's okay.

We as women are bestowed with a unique feminine energy, the potent power that nurtures life. Yet, in our fast-paced world, we often find ourselves caught up in the whirlwind of responsibilities, expectations, and societal pressure. We often neglect this innate energy and the need for balance, well-being, and wholeness. From personal experience, I know how this can lead to a disconnect, loss of authenticity, and a struggle to maintain health and happiness.

The essence of self-care and holistic well-being can easily get overshadowed amidst the chaos. However, within every woman resides an innate wisdom that longs to be heard, a calling from her soul urging her to reconnect with her authentic self, to nourish her body and spirit, and to radiate love, grace, and vitality.

Unfortunately, women have been conditioned to believe that self-love and self-care is selfish, and that self-sacrifice is virtuous. I'm telling you right now that this mindset is damaging. It's about finding a balance between the two and getting the help you need to feel whole. Self-care takes practice, and having a bubble bath occasionally doesn't count. If you're thinking right now, I'm too busy for self-care, even more reason to be reading this book. To begin a new routine involving self-care, a mindset change must be made. Self-care is as important as getting to work on time or making sure your children's lunches are packed. If you have time to watch a show or check social media feeds, you have time to look after your personal needs.

As a woman, in many ways you are the backbone of your world. You may be a mother, daughter, sister, partner, friend, and a professional. You juggle numerous roles and responsibilities each day and do it exceptionally well most of the time. Yet, despite your incredible strength and resilience, you may feel overwhelmed, stressed, disconnected, and physically and emotionally exhausted.

One of the significant issues you may be facing is the pressure to have it all — a thriving career, a happy family, a vibrant social life, and a perfect body. The societal expectation to excel in every area can be a tremendous burden. This constant push to achieve and maintain these standards can make you feel perpetually stressed and unsatisfied, causing emotional and physical pain.

The problem is exacerbated by our modern lifestyle, often characterized by long work hours, high-stress environments, poor nutrition, and inadequate physical activity. You may be so busy caring for others that you fully neglect your personal health and well-being, leading to fatigue, weight gain, hormonal imbalances, and mood swings. These will impact your quality of life, affect your relationships, and leave you feeling depleted and frustrated.

Moreover, the lack of time and space for self-care and relaxation can lead to chronic stress and anxiety. Over time, these conditions can precipitate more severe health issues like heart disease, diabetes, obesity, as well as autoimmune conditions and mental health disorders. You may find yourself looking for a quick fix with a pill or drug but find it doesn't get to the root of the problem and that you are not truly happy or fulfilled despite having everything on the surface.

As women, it can be challenging to show self-love, self-care or overcome a lack of self-worth. You may not feel you deserve self-love and self-care. Being self-assertive is showing your willingness to stand up for yourself, who you are, and being treated with kindness and respect. Once you've decided to make self-care a priority, guard your time as if it's the most valuable gem in the world. It is your time, and it is precious.

Many of us were shamed during childhood by our families, in school, or in organized religious settings. We were taught to go along with the masses to avoid conflict, and our attempts at self-assertion were met with humiliation and put-downs. I can relate to what author Bell Hooks writes in her book, *All About Love: New Visions*. She courageously calls attention to the idea that, *"Sexist socialization teaches females that self-assertiveness is a threat to our femininity."* She suggests that embracing this flawed reasoning sets the stage for diminished self-worth, highlighting that the apprehension of asserting oneself often emerges in women who have been conditioned to conform as good girls or dutiful daughters.

I can certainly relate, for in my own patriarchal childhood home I was faced with punishment for speaking my mind or "talking back." Even still, I was a rebel at heart. I always wanted to understand the why of things and often questioned my father, only to find myself grounded for weeks at a time for doing so. When I would inquire about the "why" of things, the response I received was "because I told you so".

I learned it wasn't safe to ask questions, express myself, my thoughts, feelings, or opinions. So rather than asserting what I thought or felt at the appropriate time, I would either lash out rebelliously or say whatever I thought would please my dad by withholding truths and suppressing my true thoughts.

I found it exhausting to be met with a brick wall when I shared my thoughts or felt that my mother or I were being mistreated and unjustly manipulated and controlled. I began to hold onto my anger, but it would often reveal itself at the slightest trigger. In those moments, I would defend my voice or anyone close to me with a fierceness that was startling.

If you're anything like me and many other women I know, you may have found yourself in similar situations. In silencing yourself, you may be harboring resentment and/or experiencing a disconnection from your true self, leading to a sense of unfulfillment and loss of purpose.

In addition to physical and emotional struggles you may have experienced due to suppressing your self-assertiveness, you may also be grappling with a sense of spiritual disconnection. With societal norms emphasizing external achievements, there's often little room for inner growth and exploration of your spiritual self.

While it's normal to experience these challenges, the reality is that living in constant stress and disconnection isn't healthy or sustainable. It's time to break this cycle. You deserve MORE, and in this lifetime, you deserve to feel vibrant, balanced, and fulfilled physically, emotionally, and spiritually, but it's up to you to make that happen. This is where Sacred Self: A Journey to Embracing Feminine Wholeness guides you through a transformative journey toward total health and well-being.

As you dig deeper into the chapters of this book, you will learn about the importance of clean eating. Understanding how to nourish your body with wholesome foods can improve your energy levels, enhance your immune system, promote weight balance, and even balance your hormones. You will also explore the importance of reducing the toxins in your diet, your environment, and create awareness around products you use that can interfere with your health and well-being.

Another substantial aspect of this journey is the emphasis on movement, exercise, and breathing techniques. By recognizing the significance of consistent physical activity, involving gentle movement and yoga, you can acquire strategies to integrate exercise into your daily routine. This has the potential to enhance physical health, boost strength and stamina, elevate mood and mental clarity, and contribute to an overall sense of well-being.

The book also guides you in creating a sanctuary in your home, a sacred space that is a haven for relaxation and rejuvenation. The resulting sense of tranquility and order can bring about a reduction in stress levels and a heightened sense of well-being.

Nourishing spiritual wellness is also a key aspect of this book. This section offers tools to reconnect with your inner self, reduce stress, enhance mental clarity, and boost emotional resilience. This in-depth understanding will help you develop personal practices, leading to a stronger mind-body connection, better stress management, and deeper inner peace.

Another unique benefit comes from the exploration of healing with earth stones, providing knowledge to harness the power of crystals for healing and balance. Understanding how to incorporate crystals into your daily life can offer new self-care and energy management avenues.

Emotional well-being and mental health are also addressed in this guide, offering practical strategies for maintaining emotional balance and building resilience and inner strength. The chapters on cultivating positive relationships and personal growth offer valuable insights for building supportive relationships and aligning your life with your values.

The final chapters focus on the power of gratitude and affirmations, key practices that can fundamentally shift your perspective on life. Understanding and applying these principles can increase positivity, improve mental health, enhance resilience, and a greater sense of fulfillment.

In essence, this book is not merely a book—it's a transformational tool that empowers you to take charge of your well-being. Its benefits are comprehensive, designed to bring about a holistic transformation that resonates in every aspect of your life. It invites you to embark on a journey toward a healthier, happier, and more balanced life—a journey that every woman deserves to make.

My personal journey has given me insights and experiences that make me uniquely qualified to guide you on this path. I understand the struggles, challenges, and rewards because I've been there. I am certainly not perfect by any means, none of us are, but the point is we must remind ourselves that as humans we are ALL imperfect. Even as I write this, I sometimes find myself neglecting my own self-care and need to set reminders to take breaks to nourish myself with what I need. We are all works in progress, and we can enjoy the ride or fight it. Be patient and loving with yourself and give yourself the care you need.

I am not just offering you a book but a compassionate hand and a proven roadmap to guide you toward reclaiming your health, embracing wholeness, and living the vibrant life you deserve. I can guide you not from a distant theoretical perspective but from a place of empathy, understanding, and firsthand experience. If you're a woman feeling overwhelmed by the pressures of modern life and yearning for balance, wellness, and a connection to your authentic self, this is the book for you.

So, take a long deep breath right now (or three) and take the first step toward the most fulfilling journey you've ever embarked on. It's time to reclaim your health, embrace your feminine power, and live a life of balance and fulfillment. Don't wait another moment. Turn the page and let your journey to returning to your sacred self and embracing feminine wholeness begin today.

While you're reading this, you'll notice journal prompts at the end of each chapter. It's helpful to have a journal and pen with you while reading so you can do some soul inquiring along the way.

"In the darkness, she found parts of her that made her the brightest." – Spirit Daughter (www.spiritdaughter.com)

1

Introduction to caring for your Sacred Self

    I prioritize self-care as a vital and non-negotiable part of my daily life, nourishing my mind, body, and soul with love and compassion.

A vital part of the female experience is finding ways to cultivate wholeness. Health (physical, emotional, and spiritual) is part of a woman's story, consistently addressed in spiritual practices, holistic health, and wellness.

Healthy living is not just the absence of disease or illness; it is a sense of wholeness that allows you to be deeply rooted in life. To embody wholeness means to integrate and harmonize all aspects of one's being—physical, emotional, mental, and spiritual—creating a unified and balanced presence in the world. Doing this connects you with your purpose while feeling grounded and connected. This process can involve appreciating all aspects of yourself, including your physical, spiritual, and social selves. It involves developing a balanced relationship between your mind, body, and spirit as well as your relationship with others. This way, you connect with everything: accepting your **past**, being **present**, and shaping your **future**.

Connecting to the wholeness of the divine feminine self is a lifelong journey. It's a relationship; constantly being tended to. Like any relationship, it really must be maintained and nourished consistently to ensure your healthy lifestyle remains intact. This can be challenging at times when you're juggling work, home-life balance, and have an endless list of tasks and responsibilities.

Sometimes you may find there is no time however. Be patient with yourself. If you have children or have a demanding career, do everything you can to carve out some time in your day (even if it's just 15 minutes in the morning or in the evening before bed) for nurturing your mind, body, and spirit. You may even rub off on your children and spouse in a positive way. What a gift to give to yourself and to them when they see the positive changes in you and see the positive healthy habits they can learn to implement in their own lives.

The key for women is finding ways to move past damaging limiting beliefs about ourselves and the world around us to live with greater self-love, acceptance, self-nurturance, and self-care. This starts by becoming more aware of what we're doing that has the potential to harm us, learning to trust our intuition and begin relearning healthier ways of doing things.

What we feed our minds and bodies WILL affect us physically and emotionally. Be conscious of what you feed yourself with. From the negativity in the news, to comparing yourself to the perceived perfection of others in social media, to the movies we watch and the music you listen to, along with what we put IN and ON your body, you can inadvertently overload your system with toxicity. Instead choose to feed your mind and body with what it needs to feel nourished and whole.

Working on embracing wholeness does not have to be a monumental project. Instead, it can be a simple process to commit to in the moment with action and intent by breathing, relaxing, connecting with your inner wisdom, and nourishing yourself. Embracing your wholeness involves actively participating in this process at various stages of your life.

I find it helpful to listen to a music playlist throughout my day while I work, walk, drive, exercise, cook, clean, read, etc. It helps me feel empowered, balanced, and helps keep me motivated. Many women find it helpful to create a music playlist of their own or find one that centers them. I love the Divine Goddess Mix and the Queen B's Girl Power Mix on Spotify but find a mix, or create your own that motivates YOU to move, elevate your mood, and/or de-stress.

The Importance of Self-Care for Women

Caring for your "self" is not only a fundamental aspect of your individualized well-being, it's also a crucial step in an individual's overall wellness. When you embrace wholeness, you can better contribute to society and reach your full potential as a human being. Establishing a healthy self-care routine is one of the most important things women can do for themselves.

A vital aspect of embracing wholeness for women is developing the awareness that you are more than just your physical presence on this planet. Your physical body is obviously important, but if you ONLY focus on your physical body, you can lose sight of nurturing your mind and spirit. We must all look deeper.

Embracing wholeness is an active process of self-nurturance and balancing all three—mind, body and spirit. However, many of us have suffered a life-changing event, a personal health scare or an emotional breakdown before we choose to truly look deeper.

Sometimes we are thrust into change, regardless of how fervently we avoid it or how uncomfortable it makes us. I am guilty of this myself. I look back at my life and reflect on times when I was complacent and resisted change, even when change was what I needed more than anything. If that's you, you are NOT alone.

Show patience towards yourself and steer clear of engaging in negative self-talk. One of the most significant truths of embracing wholeness is that if your body is healthy, you are more able to express yourself in ways that might have been even more difficult if we couldn't maintain that well-being. You can be free and open with your body and spirit if you're healthy mentally and physically.

When you're open, you can be responsible for your own healing process. This is where the journey begins. Join me in finding your feminine wholeness.

1. Physical Health: Maintaining good physical well-being is essential for women to prevent various health conditions. Regular movement, a balanced diet, and sufficient sleep all contribute to maintaining a healthy weight, reducing the chronic diseases risks such as heart disease, diabetes, osteoporosis, and certain cancers. Physical activity enhances cardiovascular health, strengthens bones and muscles, improves overall energy levels, and helps reduce the risk of anxiety and depression. It enhances blood flow and helps reduce pain and discomfort.

Physically active women are also more likely to have a considerably lower body fat percentage, which can result in a lower risk for heart disease and diabetes. Physical activity doesn't have to mean running a marathon or working out for hours a day (unless you love doing those things). It can mean things as simple as going for a walk in nature, swimming, doing squats while brushing your teeth, deep breathing while driving (eyes on the road though, please), or yoga breathing techniques while waiting for your coffee to brew. It can also mean stretching and meditating in bed, or receiving holistic treatments like massage and reflexology. Even 20 minutes a day can make a difference. Whatever it is, it should be something you enjoy and not something you dread. Dig deeper to find out what that is for you.

2. Mental Health: Women often juggle multiple roles and responsibilities, increasing stress levels and potential mental health challenges. Healthy living practices such as regular movement, stress management techniques (e.g., meditation, deep breathing exercises), and adequate sleep can significantly improve mental well-being. Prioritizing self-care, seeking social support, and maintaining healthy work-life balance are essential for keeping stress low and promoting mental wellness.

3. Reproductive Health: Women's reproductive health is unique and requires particular attention. Monitoring what you feed your body and what you put on your body can impact reproductive health, fertility, and pregnancy outcomes. Regular gynecological check-ups, practicing safe sex, and utilizing contraception effectively are crucial. A balanced diet, exercise, and avoiding harmful substances like tobacco and excessive alcohol and limiting other toxin exposures are vital for optimal reproductive health.

4. Social and Emotional Well-Being: Maintaining feminine wholeness is essential for positive emotional and social well-being. Discovering where you might be suppressing emotions, past hurts, and trauma can help process those emotions to forgive and let go. This can enhance your ability to feel empathy, which is critical for maintaining positive relationships with yourself and others. Physical and mental wellness is vital for promoting your inner wisdom, empathy, and love so you can transform negative emotions into positive ones. They also play a crucial role in fostering self-esteem, which can help you show more compassion, as opposed to judgment, and show up more confident and comfortable in social interactions, your home, and workplace.

5. Professional/Career Development: Embracing wholeness can enhance career opportunities and success. Since workplace demands of women include more multitasking, working long hours and juggling family responsibilities, adopting a healthy lifestyle and a self-care routine that supports career development and boosts productivity can result in a happier, more fulfilled work experience.

Tapping into your feminine wisdom and intuition can also help you connect with your life's purpose and eventually lead to a fulfilling career you're passionate about. When you tap into a higher purpose and begin to manifest your dreams, you create beautiful things.

6. Hormonal Changes: Women experience a multitude of hormonal changes throughout life — menstruation, pregnancy, and menopause to name a few. From personal experience, I know first-hand how these transitions can bring about physical and emotional challenges.

For some women, symptoms are so severe that seeking the help of an acupuncturist or functional (holistic or integrative) physician can help ease their symptoms and get to the issue's root cause, instead of just treating symptoms with medications.

I struggled for many years after discontinuing birth control with severe menstrual cramps, uterine fibroids, bladder issues, painful sex, dryness, and urinary pain. As my body gradually moved into menopause, my symptoms were just as horrible until I got the help of a natural doctor, acupuncturist, and therapist.

It took time to find the right balance of supplements, diet, and addressing emotional blocks but it finally paid off. That doesn't mean that I never experience any of the symptoms I previously experienced, but they have drastically diminished, and healing my body has given me the ability to actively work on my thinking to help me feel energized, enlivened, and seeking a higher purpose.

7. Pain Management: Chronic pain often requires a multi-faceted approach to alleviate symptoms and resolve the underlying root causes. Root cause is the key here. Oftentimes in Western medicine, doctors find they don't have time to advise on nutrition, exercise, and supplementation. Not only do they not have time, that's not what they're specifically trained to do. They're trained to treat symptoms, often through pharmaceuticals, but not get to the root cause and prevention.

This isn't because there isn't a desire to do so, it's more that there's too little time. However, the problem with solely addressing chronic symptoms and not getting to the root cause is that when only treated with pharmaceuticals to ease symptoms, it can cause other symptoms and side effects in the long run.

By avoiding the root cause and only addressing symptoms, over time you may find yourself taking an increasing number of medications, potentially creating more illness and side effects. It's like a snowball that is increasingly difficult to escape. Addressing an acute issue is one thing; we need our doctors to help ease immediate symptoms (a break, cut, or blunt trauma), but using pharmaceuticals to treat chronic symptoms can be a dangerous game. Harm from medication may not appear until several years later, so it's important to be an active participant in managing your health.

The human body has an incredible capacity for healing and self-regulation. Our bodies possess various physiological mechanisms that work to repair and maintain balance. In many cases, given the right conditions, our body can heal itself from injuries, illnesses, and imbalances. A well-balanced diet, regular movement, and adequate sleep help reduce stress levels, relieve fatigue, and depression. They also improve overall immune function to maximize the body's ability to self-heal.

8. Longevity and Aging: Healthy living habits adopted early in life significantly impact long-term health and aging. Women generally have a longer life expectancy than men, and healthy lifestyle choices contribute to healthy aging. Regular movement, a balanced diet rich in nutrients, maintaining a healthy weight, and avoiding harmful habits (smoking is perhaps the best example), can reduce the risk of age-related diseases and promote independence and vitality in later years.

Being strong and independent in your elder years is key. Just living longer doesn't mean you have quality of life. Living a fulfilling, quality life LONGER is what we all strive for.

9. Disease Prevention: Healthy living can significantly reduce the risk of diseases that disproportionately affect women, such as breast cancer, cervical cancer, and osteoporosis. Regular screenings, self-examinations, and healthy lifestyle choices are critical in early detection and prevention.

The Connection Between Feminine Energy and Wellness

Feminine energy is a life force, or prana that flows through all living systems. In the physical world, feminine energy is often perceived as "vital" and "life-giving," while masculine energy is known as "tough," "energizing," and "concentrated." Your feminine genius is spiral or cyclical in nature, just as is the moon and your monthly cycles.

Masculine genius is linear, rational, goal-oriented and competitive. In ancient history, feminine energy was viewed as something women needed to nurture or protect. It was considered the raw material for life—the ancient form from which everything comes. This has been lost, however, in our current culture with the pressure to constantly be giving and nurturing (feminine energy) while also doing and performing (masculine energy).

We all have feminine and masculine energy in us, but sometimes we are so busy doing it ALL, yet forgetting to nurture ourselves, creating a feeling of deadness, disconnect and numbness.

Thankfully, we're seeing a rise in the sacred feminine more than any other period in our lifetimes. In ancient times, every woman was seen as sacred, not something to be silenced, controlled, or suppressed. This does not mean that you're being called to rise above men, but to bring about a balance between masculine and feminine energies.

Feminine energy is a vital component of overall wellness and well-being. It is linked to the energies of the heart, voice, intuition, compassion, and unconditional love. Feminine energy is also associated with your ability to nurture yourself and others, contributing significantly to your social, emotional, physical, and spiritual health. When you cultivate a relationship with your feminine energy, you begin to feel more connected with others — a knowing that can carry over into all aspects of your life.

Feminine energy emphasizes the importance of self-care and nurturing oneself. Women tend to have a natural inclination toward caring for others but often overlook their own well-being. Embracing feminine energy involves recognizing the need for self-care practices. Regular relaxation, engaging in activities that bring joy, setting boundaries, and prioritizing one's physical and mental health all contribute to wholeness.

Being in touch with your feminine energy can help you become more grounded and present-oriented, leading to greater happiness, fulfillment, and health.

Cultivating the feminine involves recognizing that various aspects of life are interconnected. This does not mean women must do everything men do or that you must conform to traditional, gender-based societal roles. Instead, it is about recognizing your unique connection with the world and others.

Looking inward and asking yourself deeply what areas of your life may be out of balance, or may be causing resentment, fear, frustration, or anger requires some time to self-reflect in order to address them.

Tapping into your feminine energy promotes finding balance and embracing life's natural ebb and flow. Embracing feminine energy encourages you to honor and listen to your energy levels, set realistic goals, and be patient in forging new paths while remaining true to your passion and purpose.

Feminine energy acknowledges and values the importance of emotional well-being. Women may experience a wider range of emotions due to hormonal and societal factors. I certainly know that has been the case for me. But I have learned that embracing and expressing emotions healthily is essential for overall wellness. This may involve emotional self-awareness, seeking emotional support from loved ones or therapists, engaging in creative outlets, and finding healthy ways to manage stress. For me, that entailed all the above.

By understanding that feminine energy is both a physical and spiritual aspect of your health and wellness, we as women can begin to feel more empowered in making a difference in our health.

I couldn't agree more with LiYana Silver, as she asserts in her book, *Feminine Genius* that *"The root cause of the world's suffering is that women are dimmed down, stressed-out and burned-out."* She describes women as candle flames, dazzling sources of light and fire, but most of us are dimmed way down and become barely a flicker. She contends that the women who will help light, lead, and heal our world do the radical act of turning their own inner flame back on.

I add to this that not only can you turn your own flame on again using your feminine genius, but you can also help light the torches of other women with your own torch. So often women spend so much time self-bashing or cutting other women down, but what would happen if we instead diverted our attention to our own healthy body, mind, reinvigorated sensuality, a sense of self-love, an act of creativity, an intentionally formed family, community service or helping others?

Our Approach to caring for your Sacred Self

Sacred self-care is not a one-size-fits-all proposition. Every woman is different, having different needs and specific goals. If the term self-care makes you cringe, as it once did for me and does for many other women, even more reason to read this book.

The goal is to live life fully, finding fulfillment and balance in each step you take. As important as it is to be healthy physically, mental and emotional well-being are just as crucial for positive health outcomes. For women, these are often overlooked, leading to missteps toward a healthier lifestyle. It is essential to understand that healthy living aims not to get to a completely "perfect" body or unrealistically live in a state of bliss, but to feel that life is a gift and should be fulfilling, even through life's ups and downs. Remember that the downs are temporary and commit to nurturing yourself with self-care during them. That's when we need self-care the most.

Self-care practices are simple but not always easy. It takes consistency, diligence, and dedication to change one's health positively. However, try not to see living with wholeness as too tricky or too much to ask for. Sacred self-care is about nurturing your body and making minor changes to your lifestyle over time—changes you can sustain over the long-term.

Sacred self-care starts with a mindset of openness and willingness to try new things while also remaining receptive to old ideas that may have been previously dismissed by society, or previous life or childhood experiences. There is no wrong way to be healthy; embracing wholeness means you look at all aspects of your health holistically, including mind, body, and spirit. This means you respect the entire system and its parts whenever you make a change.

Health benefits can result from a synergy of physical and mental symptoms, emotions, behaviors, and responses. Just recognizing that your mental health (worry, anger, stress, disconnection) affects your physical health is a step to get you closer to improving your overall well-being. When symptoms overlap across body systems and relate to one another in an integrated manner, they can provide greater insight into the causes of illness and guide practitioners in making specific interventions more effective.

Embracing wholeness is not about being perfect or 100% healthy daily; instead, it is about always tending to your body, mind, and spirit to live fully. It's about truly listening to your body and learning how to balance life's challenges with time to rest, de-stress, and tend to yourself. As women, we're often so busy nurturing others and neglect our own needs. We must remember to fill our own cups too. If your cup is empty, there isn't much left to pour into the cups of others. Throughout this book, you will find affirmations at the beginning of each chapter. I encourage you to repeat some of them over and over to help re-wire your brain. You will also find journal prompts to complete at the end of each chapter. Here's your first.

Journal Prompt:

How have you shown up and cared for yourself in times of need, change, or turmoil?

Do you often put others first? If so, what can you do to make minor changes to prioritize your own self care, especially during hard times?

2

Embracing Feminine Energy

> ❝ *I embrace my feminine power, expressing love and grace in every aspect of my life.*

Women are more than just biological specimens. We are inseparable from the planet, our children, and everything around us. Embracing our femininity can be challenging however, especially when we are influenced by a variety of societal, cultural, and personal factors. Societal expectations, cultural conditioning, internalized stereotypes, media influence, fear of judgement, pressure to confirm to masculine norms, personal trauma, heartbreak, and or a lack of positive role models can keep us from expressing our femininity authentically.

Many of us feel pressured to conform to societal expectations, leading to a sense of inadequacy if we do not align with conventional feminine ideals. Cultural influences also play a significant role in shaping our perceptions of femininity. Some cultures may have rigid expectations regarding how women should behave, dress, or express themselves, making it challenging to embrace a more diverse and authentic sense of feminine power. As a result, we might internally stereotype femininity by associating it solely with traits like passivity, nurturing, or emotional sensitivity which can create conflict when we possess qualities that deviate these narrow definitions. Moreover, many women fear being judged or perceived as too assertive, not nurturing enough, or not conforming to societal expectations, which can lead to self-censorship. On top of it all, media portrayals of femininity often emphasize narrow beauty standards and unrealistic ideals that create insecurities within us.

Then there's heartbreak, loss, or disappointment that have led many women to engage in self-protective behaviors. Many of us, including myself, have found ourselves creating distance from traditionally feminine qualities because we feared being hurt, shamed, misunderstood and or truly heard. Putting up the proverbial wall around our hearts can harden us and WILL prevent us from being able to trust and lead with empathy.

There's still time to embrace the real you and be free of self-imposed restrictions that limit you from who you could be. It all starts with understanding what your "real" self is and what healthy feminine energy feels like. My hope is that you will look at yourself in a new light by recognizing how society shapes women into what it wants them to be, instead of what they truly are inside.

Understanding Feminine Energy

Feminine energy is powerful, nurturing, life-giving, and a source of connection. It is the birth-giver and the sustainer of life. Women are nurturers at their core; they give birth to children and watch them grow into adulthood through their formative years. They share in the joys and sorrows. Even if you're a woman like me, who has never personally given birth, you have the ability to nurture. Whether it be nurturing a child, an idea or a creation like a book or piece of art, our nature is to nurture. A woman's strength is in her ability to create, giving birth to new beginnings for herself or someone else.

When feminine energy flows within, you are whole, the yin to balance your masculine yang. All women have a balance of masculine and feminine within. But when your feminine energy is blocked due to stress from society or your own imposed self-preservation, it can lead to depression, illness, and pain.

Feminine energy is a powerful force in the universe. It is a part of the interdependence of nature and life. Feminine energy is rooted in wisdom, creativity, and honor. A woman's voice is essential to society's growth and productivity. To embrace your feminine energy, it's crucial to learn how to listen to your intuition to know who you truly are. A woman can learn to develop her intuition through life experiences, meditation, and stillness to guide her in the right direction.

There are so many resources available to help you on your journey to wholeness and fulfillment. Remember to love your feminine self and surround yourself with people who love, care, and respect you for the person that you are. Surround yourself with beings who will nurture the real you, without holding you back from becoming the best version of yourself. Seek people who will cheer you on, not hold you down.

When a woman embraces her feminine energy, she becomes more connected to the world, not just to the people she's directly surrounded by. Intuition IS your strongest guide; when you listen to it and trust it, you'll learn how to navigate life's obstacles and challenges with grace, peace, and inner confidence.

Embracing your feminine energy involves listening so your intuition can guide you to health, wholeness, and well-being for yourself and those you care for. This involves communicating with the feminine energy within to become fully aware of the feminine genius within you.

Here are some forgotten truths about embodying your feminine genius:

1. Your mind is not the smartest thing about you.
2. Your body is wildly intelligent and divine.
3. Passion and intuition are held in your body.

These truths help you **keep your flame lit!** When you learn to listen to your body, you understand that even if you want to live in your head and overthink to the point of overwhelm or the opposite, which is avoidance, suppression, denial or disconnection from reality, your body will signal that something is wrong. No matter how much we want to avoid an issue, it WILL come out in our bodies, whether we like it or not!

How many times have you known a woman who held things in or always pushed through or became so hardened, angry, and resentful that she eventually become seriously ill to the point she could no longer avoid what might be happening in her life? I've recognized this within myself numerous times after suffering heartbreak, built walls around myself, fearing true intimacy and suppressing my feelings, to over time become ill with chronic joint pain, headaches, and chronic bladder issues. I witnessed this in my mother when she became overwhelmed with severe migraines after 15 years of denying her own needs. I've witnessed this in numerous girlfriends as well. It became an ah hah! moment for me when I finally saw the correlation.

A woman using her feminine energy will understand that she is ONLY in control of her own emotions and cannot control or be responsible for the emotions of others. Once we come to terms with this fact, we can learn to positively transform our own thoughts and emotions. But it takes awareness and practice. Remind yourself of this, as if it were a mantra, if you find yourself wanting to manipulate, change or mold the emotions and actions of others into what you want them to be.

As much as we may resist embracing these truths, women are not meant to live within a box of society's creation or restrictions against who we truly are. Consciously balancing feminine energy means recognizing there is no such thing as orgasmic utopia. We must realize that balance is a state of being. When you embrace your feminine genius, you take complete control over your life and decisions while setting boundaries to be treated with kindness and respect, not only by others but by ourselves as well.

The Importance of a Healthy Feminine Energy

When you embrace your full potential and identity, you can achieve a healthy balance for yourself, others, and the world around you. When you have an open heart, listen, and pay attention, it leads your soul to peace within. Healthy feminine energy compels a woman to understand her power as a pure being of light. Her light shines brightly within her spirit, reflected through her beauty, patience, and grace. Spirit and body are held in divine union through this energy.

Playfulness comes from giving yourself permission to see the humor in life's challenges without taking things too seriously. Honesty comes from a willingness to honestly look at yourself and share your experience with others you trust. When a woman is free of self-doubt and self-imposed restrictions, she is confident while remaining compassionate toward others and avoids passing judgment, inwardly or outwardly.

Here's another truth: you can't hear your own inner truth (feminine wisdom) if you're too high up on your high horse! As you start to allow your light to shine brightly, avoid the urge to pass judgment on others. We don't have to steal the torches of others to keep our flames lit. You can use your own torch to help light others' torches along the way.

Feminine energy is rooted in your focus and connection to the world. Having the ability to hear your self-talk without allowing negative self-talk to take over, you'll begin to listen to your soul's calling as an essential tool providing motivation, encouragement, direction, and inspiration.

Your feminine genius is allowing yourself to feel emotion by acknowledging your feelings and listening to your inner truth. This is trusting the voice of your soul.

Balancing Masculine and Feminine Energies

Balancing masculine and feminine energies involve recognizing and integrating both qualities within you. Extreme behavior or repression of one or the other is a certain road to trouble. Both sets of qualities are necessary for your fulfilment as a human being. We need the whole spectrum of masculine and feminine energies within to find balance.

We all have both masculine and feminine characteristics within ourselves. How you express those characteristics defines your individuality and makes you who you are. When you embrace both sets of characteristics within yourself, you learn to balance them for the betterment of yourself and those around you.

The balance that occurs when both sets of traits come together helps make up for any weaknesses in one set by drawing on the strengths of another. These energies are often described as complementary forces that work together to create a greater whole within you.

How Are Masculine and Feminine Energies Interconnected?

Masculine and feminine energies interconnect through thoughts, feelings, and dreams interdependently within each of us, regardless of gender. They complement and balance each other, playing a vital role in various aspects of human life, relationships, and personal growth. Exploring and integrating both masculine and feminine qualities enhances personal growth. Balancing action-oriented (masculine) traits with receptivity and intuition (feminine) traits lead to a more holistic approach to life's challenges.

Many spiritual practices emphasize connecting with both masculine and feminine energies as a means of connecting to higher consciousness or divinity. For example, some traditions associate the masculine with transcendence (God) and the feminine with immanence (Goddess).

Having a balance of masculine energy within you makes you more self-motivated to achieve success. Masculine energy may provide the linear, analytical, and structured thinking needed to approach problems logically, while feminine energy swirls, contributing to creativity, intuition, and emotional intelligence to find innovative solutions.

Recognizing that masculine and feminine energies are not fixed but exist on a spectrum allows individuals to be more adaptable in different situations. This fluidity allows for personal growth and empowerment.

Having strong feminine energy within allows you to be more compassionate and to resist the urge to judge. When both energies come together, your approach will be more open, empathetic, and honest. Sometimes we're too harsh and critical about ourselves and others but try to catch yourself when going down that road. I promise you this, you will not truly experience wholeness and balance if you succumb to negativity.

By staying open-minded, asking questions, and having an open heart when listening, you more easily understand what others might be going through, and have empathy. This doesn't mean you always have to "just be nice," or "polite," adhering to societal expectations. You can be honest and communicate with kindness. People come and go in life. Sometimes those people feed the negativity and it's up to you to resist the negative temptation to participate in it. Women tend to stay quiet to keep the peace and block out negative thoughts, but when they rise, it's best to address them rather than pushing them down where they will almost certainly surface again. Ask yourself why the negative feelings are arising. Are they a result of past traumas, hurts, disappointments? Are the feelings trying to tell you something? Sit with them and ask yourself these questions before reacting. Again, you are only in control of your own emotions and actions, not the emotions or actions of others.

The power of positive thinking has gotten a lot of focus over the last several years. Unfortunately, some people have come to interpret this to mean that we should never have a negative thought or feeling. This can lead to a superficial relationship with life and relationships. When we do this, we're repressing a part of ourselves that needs to be seen, heard, and processed. Repressing parts of self or suppressing feelings often means they don't go away but become buried deep within and often come out when you least expect it.

I have been guilty of this myself and eventually it all came crashing down on me. Pushing my feelings deep down did not serve me well. Allow yourself to be human, honoring all the thoughts, feelings and moods that pass through you on a given day. Instead of blocking out negative thoughts, you can simply observe them, try to understand where they're coming from and what they're trying to teach you, then let them go. Over time it will become easier to resist negative thoughts that try to keep you captive.

For your reality to be full of peace, love, and harmony, acknowledge negative thoughts, address them, even journal about them, but then feed the good! This doesn't mean you should live in fantasy land and avoid reality; it means nourishing the goodness around you.

In a state of awareness, love and peace, bad thoughts that come to mind can quickly be overcome. Feeding bad thoughts breeds negativity, stagnation, and keeps you from reaching your heart's desires.

When we embrace feminine energy, we balance the masculine energy within. Masculine and feminine energies are not separate entities, but yin and yang that complement each other. Together they make up an androgynous whole, as opposed to an either/or perspective being more important.

A book I recently read made a significant impact on my life. I bought the book as a gift for a friend months prior to her birthday and decided I would read it first. *Rise Sister Rise*, by Rebecca Campbell brought me to an awakening and guided me to the spiritual path I'm on today. Not only did the author propel me on a path of feminine awakening, but she also helped guide me to a deeper understanding of what it means to be heard, loved, and understood with compassion for self and the support of others.

In her book, Rebecca Campbell contends, *"as we are coming out of 5,000 years of patriarchy, where the unbalanced masculine has been the focus, it is important to note that the unbalanced feminine can be just as destructive."*

The chart from her book lists some of the characteristics of the sacred masculine and feminine energies when balanced and unbalanced. I've included it here because it was an ah hah! moment for me. Read through and see which you relate to. Remember we are capable of them all.

SACRED FEMININE

Compassionate, Wise, In touch with her ability to heal, Connected with nature and her seasons, Sees herself as whole. Loves unconditionally, Fiercely protective of the planet and her children, Sexual, Wise, Knows her Power, Intuitive, Passionate, Empathetic, Understanding, Healer, Fertile, Creative, Abundant, In flow with the rest of life, Provider of Shakti, Assertive, Truth seeker, Fills up her well, Able to be supported, Revered and adored by the masculine, Able to express anger and passion.

UNBALANCED FEMININE

Depressed, Needy, Codependent, Overly sensitive, Wallowing, Self-Pitying. Bitter, Self-Doubting, Victim, People-pleaser, Good girl, Low self-esteem, Dependent, Unable to stand on own two feet, Gossip, Resentful, Doesn't want to be happy, Martyr, Selfish, Can't stand other people's happiness, Manipulative, Scheming. Controlling, Spiteful, Unable to express her needs, Insecure, Puts everyone else's needs ahead of her own, Compares self to others in thought.

SACRED MASCULINE

Strong, Protective, Worships the Feminine, Supportive, Present, Active, Proactive, Abundant, Powerful, Provider. Confident, Physical, Energized, Passionate, Heroic, Courageous, able to be Supported by the feminine, Able to surrender to and be held by the feminine, Able to love unconditionally, In touch with feelings but doesn't let them control him, Empowered, Not threatened.

UNBALANCED MASCULINE

Destroys everything in his/her path, Ruthless, Does not think of anyone but himself, The end justifies the means, Forceful, Brutal, Barbaric, Selfish, Egoistic, Sees him/herself as separate, Arrogant, Disconnected from the head up, Weak, Cruel, Disconnected from emotions, Easily threatened, Cowardly, Deceitful, Stubborn, Endures and Strives when it is time to rest, Headstrong.

Activating Your Feminine Power

The first step in activating your feminine power is often understanding what your balanced and unbalanced qualities may or may not be. As a woman, you might have a natural sense that something is missing from within yourself, which causes inner conflict that impedes the full expression of your feminine power. Once you begin to acknowledge what you're repressing or where you fall short, you can consciously act to bring these missing qualities into your life.

Often, it's the lack of these qualities within yourself that causes you to look outside yourself for someone or something to lead you to fulfillment. We often do this through spending too much time on social media, shopping, drinking, sex, drugs, working or any other addictive behaviors that increase your feel-good hormones to feed your ego. However, this can negatively manifest itself in relationships with yourself and others.

Activating your feminine power is to become aware of your feminine and masculine strengths and weaknesses. List them and create a vision for how you want your strengths to manifest in your life.

Ensure that your list includes traits that specifically reflect the qualities found within your feminine and masculine energy. Have a clear vision of how these qualities can impact your life.

Once you have created your list, read the positive qualities daily, along with your vision for how they can manifest in your life. You may also want to meditate on the qualities found within your feminine energy, repeating your sacred traits over and over, as doing this will help to open your intuition, rewire your brain, and thus allow a further understanding of where these opportunities may come from.

As Rebecca Campbell suggests, you can even record yourself reciting your positive qualities in the form of a poem and listen to it daily. I took her advice and I'm certainly glad I did. It truly helped re-wire my thinking.

Creating a vision board is another way to activate qualities in your feminine energy. You're the creator of your life, so envision what your dream life looks like. With these images in mind, create a collage of everything you would love to see in your life aligning with the qualities found in your feminine energy. This can include a fulfilling career, time for yourself, sacred self-care, your relationship with others, creating something, or serving others.

The key is to choose images that reflect the qualities found within your positive feminine and positive masculine energies and to post it somewhere visible to look at daily. To do this, you may need to ask yourself specific questions about those qualities. Where do they come from? Were they learned behaviors or part of your unique personality?

Your Relationship with the Seasons and Elements

Don't underestimate the powerful effect of seasonal awareness and how nature reminds us to bring our body back into flow. Each season brings unique energy, climate, and demands our cooperation as living custodial beings.

Being connected with the seasons is akin to tuning into the heartbeat of nature itself. Connecting to nature is a mindful acknowledgment of the cyclical rhythm that governs the world around us. We are all integral parts of this intricate dance. As the seasons transition, so do our internal landscapes — energies, emotions, and even aspirations.

Women's menstrual cycles even align with the phases of the moon. Our cycles go through four phases in four weeks, just as the moon goes through four primary phases in a month. Our hormonal fluctuations do as well. Once you align with nature's cycles, you also align with the intelligence of the natural world.

Every time you gaze up at the moon, you've likely observed its ever-changing appearance. It varies from being luminous and round, a complete celestial orb of light, to seemingly absent, concealed behind the veil of darkness. Sometimes it takes on the form of a delicate crescent in the sky, while on other occasions, it appears as if it has been cleaved in two. Surprisingly, each of these moon phases carries its own unique symbolism and significance. There are spiritual meanings behind each phase of the lunar cycle.

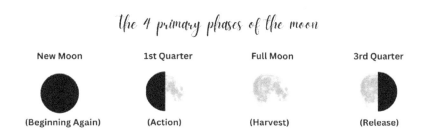

the 4 primary phases of the moon

| New Moon | 1st Quarter | Full Moon | 3rd Quarter |
| (Beginning Again) | (Action) | (Harvest) | (Release) |

1.   New Moon (Beginning Again)

Scientifically: When the sun and moon are on the same side of the Earth. Because the sun is not facing the moon, from our perspective on Earth, it looks like the dark side of the moon is facing us.

Spiritually: Think of the new moon as not only your fresh start, but your time of retreat — a time when you can regain your strength to begin again. The themes surrounding the new moon are new beginnings, fresh starts, and clean slates. Use this time for an intense reboot. Envision yourself recharging under the energy of a new moon. Mentally throw all unwanted thoughts and ineffective patterns into the trash. As you release yourself from the grip of the past, plant the seed of something new. Make a wish, set an intention, or make the decision to begin a new project. All a new moon wants you to do is start again.

2. First Quarter Moon (Action)

Scientifically: The first quarter moon meaning is often called the first-quarter phase, which occurs a week after the new moon phase. It is the first half-moon after the new moon and therefore, referred to as the first-quarter phase, which is when the moon has completed a quarter of its monthly cycle of lunar phases.

Spiritually: Because the first quarter moon occurs a week after the new moon, this is when you may start to feel some resistance in the form of obstacles. If your intentions were planted during the new moon, your first hurdles at achieving these goals are experienced here. The themes surrounding this moon are challenges, decisions, and action. Your week of rest and intention-setting is over, and now you may feel inspired to work harder. No matter how hard it gets, remember the intention you set during the last new moon and make decisions with it in mind.

3. Full Moon (Harvest)

Scientifically: A full moon occurs when the sun and the moon are on opposite sides of the Earth. Because the sun is directly across from the moon, the light completely illuminates it, making the moon appear completely full on Earth.

Spiritually: Because the sun and the moon are opposing each other, they are also in opposite zodiac signs. This brings heightened tension as you fight to find balance between two extremes. Emotions can definitely run high during this period as you struggle to come to terms with everything you're feeling. However, the full moon is also a moment of revelation, reward, and of course, change. This is when the results of all your hard work are revealed. The seed you planted on the new moon has blossomed and bloomed, making itself ready to be harvested. A powerful climax to a story that began on the new moon takes place.

4. Last Quarter (Release)

Scientifically: The last quarter moon is the reverse process of the first quarter. After a full moon, the moon wanes and becomes smaller. Now, the moon appears like a half-slice of lemon.

Spiritually: The themes surrounding this moon are release, letting go, and forgiveness. Like the moon gradually letting go of its size, you may be ready to let go of all the baggage you've been carrying. Throughout the month, you may have experienced many challenges. It's under this moon that you will let go of things like grudges, anger, and regret. Set down anything that feels too heavy and pointless to continue carrying.

Humans have used the powers of nature to magically transform their energy as long as we've been on this earth. A big part of working with nature's magic is learning how to honor cycles of the earth and connecting to the power and magic of the sun, moon, seasons, elements, and directions.

The moon is said to be feminine energy, illuminating, expressing, magnetizing, receiving, and cyclical in nature. The moon's magic is incredibly powerful. It controls the ebb and flow of the tides and helps connect with your intuition. It helps bring you home if you pay attention. The sun is known as masculine energy — hot, bright, inspiring, and a source of light energy that helps things to grow, energize, cleanse, and revitalize.

As feminine beings, it's important to remember that nature loves her cycles, which includes darkness and light. Examples are falling, death, rebirth, and repeat. Death = fall/winter, and rebirth = spring/summer. Seasons of death and rebirth are part of life.

This connection offers profound perspectives on impermanence, encouraging us to embrace change and adapt gracefully. From the rebirth of spring to the fullness of summer, the shedding of autumn, and the introspection of winter, each season brings its own lessons and energies to absorb.

Think about this for a moment. Do you find that the seasons affect your emotional and physical state? Are you aware of them, or do you find yourself resisting them as I did for most of my life?

I've learned that when you attune yourself to the natural seasonal shifts, you align your life with the earth's rhythms, deepening your sense of belonging and allowing yourself to flow harmoniously with the cycles of life.

In the modern world, however, we spend most of our days in brightly lit workspaces with the temperature set year-round. Many of us have become disconnected from the shifts in rhythm brought by the seasons. Our bodies become deprived of their daily dose of natural light and the grounding sensation of the raw earth beneath our feet.

Living and growing up in southern California, it's a good thing I love the sunshine and the ocean. I always have, even as a child. Born in the summer, I am a warm weather girl through and through. Spring and summer are my favorite seasons when I feel a sense of awakening energy when flowers are blooming, and the sun is shining brightly.

During the fall and winter months, I find myself avoiding the cooler months to escape somewhere sunnier. I never really understood the importance of the seasons and the necessity of winter until recently. I always just pushed through and continued as I would in the summer months. But by bypassing winter, my body missed out on the benefits of relaxation and revitalization that the darker months offer. So, by the time spring came along, I lacked the clarity, creativity, and newfound energy it brings. I didn't have the reserves I needed to show up as my best self, which led me to feel depleted and stressed.

Adapting self-care practices to align with the cycle of the seasons can help us to navigate transitions more smoothly. For example, self-care in the winter may focus on warmth, nourishment, and rest, while self-care in the summer may emphasize outdoor activities, hydration, and sun protection.

The changing seasons remind us of the inherent beauty in impermanence, encouraging acceptance, adaptability, and an appreciation for the cyclical nature of life. As the earth continues its orbit around the sun, marking a shift into the darker seasons, take a moment to breathe into the autumnal mood, embracing memories and quieter emotions. Whether you are in a season of personal transition, aligning with the energy of this time can guide you toward the lessons of letting go, paving the way for a rebirth on the other side. Consider the essential question: What is it time to release?

The diagram here shows the seasons of transitions and how we can remind ourselves to flow with the cycles of life.

SEASONS OF TRANSITIONS

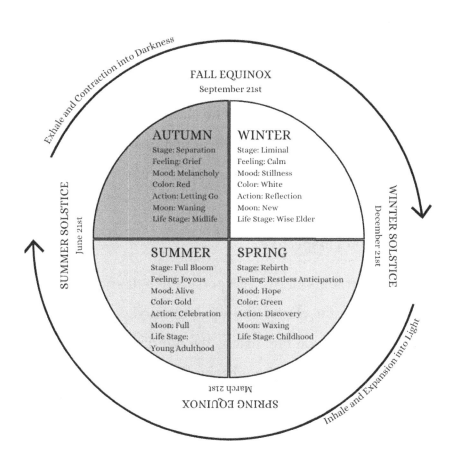

In addition to the seasons, the four classical elements of nature—earth, water, air, and fire—offer profound lessons that can inspire personal growth, self-discovery, and a deeper understanding of life. Some lessons we can learn from the four elements are:

Earth: Grounding and Stability

Lesson: Earth teaches us about stability and grounding. It reminds us to build a solid foundation in our lives, to stay connected to our values, and to cultivate a sense of security and rootedness.

Water: Adaptability and Flow

Lesson: Water symbolizes adaptability and flow. Like water, we should learn to adapt to different situations, navigate life's challenges with flexibility, and find our own flow in the ever-changing currents of life.

Air: Clarity and Perspective

Lesson: Air represents clarity and perspective. It encourages us to maintain mental clarity, be open-minded, and obtain a broader perspective on life. Just as the wind clears the air, we should seek clarity in our thoughts and actions.

Fire: Transformation and Passion

Lesson: Fire is a symbol of transformation and passion. It teaches us about the power of change and the importance of igniting our passions to fuel personal growth. Embrace transformation as a natural part of life.

These elemental lessons are often used to guide us toward a deeper understanding of ourselves and our connection to the natural world. Not only do they provide insights into the fundamental aspects of human experience and the cycles of life but should be deeply respected and honored.

To summarize, as women we can align with our cycles, the seasons, the sun, moon and the elements to gain clarity and provide our bodies with what we need by tuning into the natural rhythms of life. Doing this honors the interplay of energy, and fosters a holistic connection between mind, body, and nature. Ask yourself the following questions to gain insight on how you can gain awareness around them.

Journal Prompt:

What are your sacred, unbalanced, feminine and masculine traits? List them and read the positive qualities daily. How do you create healthy balance?

Are there patterns and behaviors that you need to let go of so new patterns and behaviors can be rebirthed?

How do you align with the energy and magic of the seasons? What can you do differently to harmonize with the rhythms of nature?

3

Nourishing Your Body

> *I am deserving of nourishing and balanced nutrition, fueling my body with vitality and energy.*

Nourishing your body is about taking care of yourself. It's about self-love, and it's also about doing what makes you feel good and healthy, not what society tells you to do. This concept is compelling, because today's women are expected to be so busy; they don't always take the time to maintain their health.

Again, self-care is not selfish. Nourishing body, mind and spirit means that you're providing it. You give it the essential nutrients and minerals while protecting and healing it from harm.

That said, I often read articles and posts about how toxic things, prevalent just about everywhere, affect and break down our bodies. So much of your surroundings have potentially damaging elements but beware of spending too much time obsessing over the fact that your food, water, air, makeup, skin, and hair products are full of chemicals. You can obsess to the point that you live in constant fear and become stuck, limited, confused and afraid.

Obsessive focus on the physical can easily take over your life, especially if you're in pain or have ailments. I have included three chapters in this book dedicated to taking care of the physical body because many of you must start your inner journey by looking to the physical, changing your diet and cleansing. I've dedicated the next three chapters to this because I believe it's a powerful foundation to build on, but you also need to understand who you are and develop your own abilities to tune in for a deeper understanding of self. We will cover the mental and spiritual journey beginning in Chapter 6 but for now, we'll discuss building a foundation (your physical body) and the importance of nourishing it and limiting toxins.

Establishing a Clean Eating Lifestyle

When we talk about clean eating, it means focusing on consuming whole, minimally processed foods and avoiding or minimizing processed or refined foods. It emphasizes eating foods that are as close to their natural state as possible and promoting a well-balanced, nutrient-dense diet. Clean eating is a lifestyle about making choices and learning how to eat in a way that makes you feel good and keeps you healthy.

When we eat when we're not hungry it's because we're stressed, bored or angry but it doesn't make us feel good. The magic happens when we shift caring about how we look to how we feel. We must learn how to nourish ourselves and eat for health and function instead of using food for emotional medicine. Our bodies are sacred temples so find the foods that support you in treating it that way.

Think of eating as medicine. Using food as medicine is about recognizing the powerful impact that food choices can have on our overall health and avoiding harmful or unhealthy foods and beverages — like sugar, processed foods, alcohol, toxic chemicals and artificial flavorings, fertilizers, and pesticides.

When grocery shopping, shop in the outer aisles (avoiding the middle aisles which contain highly processed foods with lots of sugar, sodium, and harmful additives and preservatives). Look at labels and opt for items with high protein, low sugar, and high fiber. Many packaged foods contain sugars which contribute to high calorie content, contain unhealthy fats, artificial flavors, coloring and sweeteners as well as preservatives and high amounts of sodium. These can all contribute to poor health, negatively affecting our hormones, energy levels and overall health outcomes.

Achieving clean eating means eliminating or seriously limiting these "junk" foods from your life, to will make room for healthier choices. This may seem like a lot to ask for some but nourishing your body and ridding it of toxins is necessary.

So how do we do this? Let's start with what you already know about food and then add more. Learning about the balance between protein, carbohydrates, and fats is important.

Balancing Macros

The balance of carbohydrates, protein, and fat are called macronutrients, or macros for short. If you're interested in learning what your macro breakdown should be, consider working with a dietician to help determine your needs.

There are also some great apps available to help you track your food intake to become more aware of what you're putting in your body. MyFitnessPal is an app I've found helpful. It can help you track a balanced diet with protein, carbs, and fats at every meal. An example of a good balance of macros in a meal includes salmon, sweet potato, and sautéed vegetables for dinner, or eggs, oats, and walnuts for breakfast. The following are basic guidelines for clean eating.

1. Protein is your friend. Fill up on lean protein and healthy fats. Aim for two to three times the recommended daily amount of protein (for women, between 0.8-1 gram per kilogram of body weight or .36 grams per pound of body weight). Increasing your protein intake will help you feel fuller longer, because your body needs additional time to digest protein. For example:

To calculate your daily protein needs:
Convert body weight to kilograms: Divide your weight in pounds by 2.2046 to get your weight in kilograms.
Multiply by the recommended protein intake range: Multiply your weight in kilograms by the appropriate protein intake factor based on your activity level.

Sedentary woman	Moderately active woman	Athlete or woman in intense training
weighing 150 pounds (68 kg) would aim for a minimum of 54.4 grams of protein per day (68 kg * 0.8 g/kg).	weighing 150 pounds might aim for 81.6 to 95.2 grams of protein per day (68 kg * 1.2-1.4 g/kg).	weighing 150 pounds might aim for 108.8 to 149.6 grams of protein per day (68 kg * 1.6-2.2 g/kg).

The best protein sources include wild-caught fish, organic chicken, grass-fed beef, organic plain Greek yogurt and cottage cheese, organic eggs, plant-based foods high in proteins like beans, lentils, nuts and seeds, quinoa, and some whole grains. Eat at least five to six servings of plant-based protein daily to optimize hormone balance.

When eating yogurt and/or kefir, be sure to look at labels. They're an excellent source of protein, but not all yogurts are created equal. The most important thing is to look out for additives and sugar used to make yogurt taste good. Some have high sugar content with artificial flavorings and fruit comparable to regular yogurt. Instead, opt for plain Greek yogurt with a high protein content of more than 15 grams per serving and add your own fruit and or a bit of honey if you need some flavor.

2. Eat healthy fats. They are essential for natural hormone production and reduced inflammation in the body. Some of the best sources of healthy fats include flaxseeds, chia seeds, avocados, almonds, and hemp seeds. Add at least two to three servings of fat to your diet each day to support hormone balance.

Other healthy fats include avocados, olives, and **healthy cooking oils**, including grapeseed oil, avocado oil, virgin olive oil (not extra virgin), refined coconut oil, ghee, and red palm oil.

It's important to keep cooking oil smoke points in mind, based on the type of cooking method you're planning to use. Opt for cooking oils with higher smoke points when frying, sautéing, or roasting, as those with low smoke points (under 350°F) may oxidize and break down under high heat, potentially generating harmful free radicals that can contribute to disease. Grapeseed oil and ghee have the highest smoke points of healthy cooking oils and are best for higher heat cooking.

Meanwhile, you can utilize healthy cooking oils with low smoke points to enhance the flavor of dips, spreads, dressings, or drizzle them over cooked dishes.

List of healthy cooking oils:

Grapeseed oil: The smoke point of grapeseed oil is relatively high, making it suitable for a wide range of cooking methods, including high-heat cooking. The smoke point of grapeseed oil typically falls in the range of 420°F to 450°F (215°C to 232°C), which is higher than many other commonly used cooking oils. Its high smoke point makes it a versatile choice for sautéing, frying, roasting, and baking. Additionally, grapeseed oil has a mild, neutral flavor, making it a popular option for cooking when you don't want the oil to impart a strong taste to your dishes.

Ghee (clarified butter): Ghee smoke point and flavor are both appropriate for high-heat cooking. It has a smoke point of 482 degrees.

Avocado oil: While avocado oil has a lower smoke point compared to the oils mentioned above (around 375°F or 190°C), it's still considered higher than some other cooking oils below. It's suitable for sautéing at medium heat, roasting, or as a finishing oil.

Coconut oil:

Refined coconut oil typically has a high smoke point and is suitable for high-heat cooking. Its smoke point is around 350°F to 450°F (175°C to 232°C), depending on the refining process and brand. This makes it suitable for frying, sautéing, and baking.

Unrefined (virgin) coconut oil: Unrefined or virgin coconut oil has a lower smoke point, usually around 350°F (175°C). While this is still suitable for most cooking methods, it's not recommended for very high-heat cooking like deep-frying.

Extra virgin coconut oil: Extra virgin coconut oil, which is less processed than refined versions, has a smoke point similar to unrefined coconut oil, around 350°F (175°C). It's best used for low- to medium-heat cooking or as a flavor enhancer in dishes.

Olive oil:

Extra virgin olive oil has a relatively low smoke point (around 320°F or 160°C), making it unsuitable for high-heat cooking. However, it's excellent for drizzling over salads, roasted vegetables, or using in low-heat cooking applications.

Virgin olive oil: Virgin olive oil, which is less processed than extra virgin olive oil, has a slightly higher smoke point, usually around 390°F to 410°F (199°C to 210°C). It can handle higher cooking temperatures than extra virgin olive oil and is suitable for light sautéing and baking.

Regular olive oil is known for its higher smoke point of 410°F to 465°F (210°C to 240°C). It's often labeled as "pure olive oil" or simply "olive oil."

Flaxseed oil: Flaxseed oil actually has a very low smoke point (around 225°F or 107°C). This is because of its high omega-3 fatty acid content. It's best used as a finishing oil, mixed into yogurt or smoothies, or in cold dishes like dressings.

Hemp oil: Hemp oil has a low smoke point (around 330°F or 165°C). It's best used as a drizzling oil for salads, vegetables, or grains.

Walnut oil: Walnut oil has a low smoke point (around 320°F or 160°C). It imparts a rich, nutty flavor and is great for drizzling over salads, roasted vegetables, or grilled meats.

Pumpkin seed oil: Pumpkin seed oil has a low smoke point (around 320°F or 160°C). It's known for its robust flavor and is often used as a finishing oil for soups, stews, or salad dressings.

Remember that while these oils offer health benefits, they are sensitive to heat and can become rancid or develop off flavors when exposed to high temperatures. Always choose an oil based on the cooking method you plan to use, and store them properly in a cool, dark place to maintain their quality.

Steer clear of heavily refined, highly processed vegetable oils (corn oil, canola oil, soybean oil, and safflower oil), commonly found in greasy foods. Also, avoid cooking oil brands that incorporate hydrogenated fats, such as margarine or vegetable shortening, as these contain high levels of trans fats, increasing the chances of heart disease and other health concerns.

When choosing butter, the best choice is real butter, one derived from grass-fed cows due to its nutrient composition, healthy fat content, and absence of synthetic additives. However, it is still a calorie-dense food and should be consumed in moderation, especially for those with specific dietary concerns or health conditions. Avoid margarine, however, because it is full of synthetic ingredients, additives, coloring and contains low quality fats.

3. Limit processed carbs. It's important to seriously minimize refined carbs such as white bread and pasta. Some individuals need to avoid foods that contain gluten, which is found in wheat and other grains. It's especially concerning if you have a family history of celiac disease (an intolerance to gluten). This autoimmune condition results in harm to the small intestine and can lead to anemia, fatigue, weight loss despite eating regularly, depression, inflammatory bowel disease, headaches, and even diabetes.

Some individuals who don't have celiac disease can still have a sensitivity to gluten. Gluten sensitivity can cause gas, abdominal pain, brain fog, fatigue, and joint pain, to name a few. The prevalence of individuals impacted by celiac disease or sensitivity to wheat or gluten has surged significantly in recent years. The number of people affected by celiac disease or sensitivity to wheat or gluten has risen sharply in recent years. The reason for this is still unknown, but some research has shown that it could have something to with how modern-day wheat is harvested.

If you suspect you may have celiac disease or gluten sensitivity, consider having medical tests done by a physician and/or try a gluten elimination diet for 30 days under a doctor's supervision, to see how your body responds.

Regardless of whether you have a gluten sensitivity or not, processed carbs with or without gluten are empty calories that don't digest fully and cause blood sugar spikes. Instead, go with whole grains such as brown rice, quinoa, buckwheat, and millet. These contain fiber that triggers insulin release, helping to remove harmful toxins from your body.

4. Eat the Rainbow. This means that the color of your food can tell a lot about its nutritional value. Eating a variety of colors is in fact a great way to ensure you're getting as many vitamins and minerals as possible. These include fresh fruit, veggies, beans, and legumes.

Your body needs these non-starchy carbs to produce energy, repair cells (skin, tissue, and organs), and maintain a healthy weight. It can be challenging to eat a broad, diverse variety of foods in your diet if you're a picky eater. It's certainly not easy to go from an unhealthy diet to a healthy one, but it's a step in the right direction. The point is to be aware of what you're eating.

Look at the food on your plate. Is it mainly brown foods? If so, make a list of fruits and vegetables you like that have a variety of rainbow colors and start to regularly incorporate them into your diet.

Fruit is a great source of nutrition, abundant in antioxidants that fight the free radicals your body creates. Antioxidants neutralize these damaging molecules. Free radicals may lead to premature aging (wrinkles), disease (cancer), and death. With the help of antioxidant-rich foods, your cells are essentially killing off bad cells and feeding the good cells for the greater good.

Fresh whole fruits are rich in fiber, promoting a sense of fullness while consuming fewer calories. Drinking fruit juices may also sound like a healthy option but it's not nearly the same as eating the whole fruit.

Fruit juices contain a lot of sugar (and often even have added sugars, flavors, food coloring and additives) without the fiber. Eating whole fruit contains fiber, which is essential for healthy digestion, controlling blood sugar, and decreasing the risk of heart disease. Did you know that a single six-ounce serving of 100% fruit juice contains approximately 15-30 grams of sugar and 60-120 calories? Over time, this combination can lead to weight gain. Read labels and look for sugar content.

Veggies are also nutrient-rich with many vitamins, minerals, and fiber. Look for a variety of colorful veggies. Potatoes are vegetables but are very starchy and loaded with carbohydrates. Adding colorful vegetables to your plate helps ensure you're adding vital nutrients to your meal.

If you just can't stand vegetables, then get yourself a great blender to make a smoothie with some organic veggies like cucumber, celery, parsley, a super greens mix with spinach, ginger, and maybe a small amount of pineapple or half a banana or other fruit to add flavor. You can also add filtered water (or organic coconut water) and blend away. This green combination greatly assists the body's detoxification process and is low in sugar (provided the amount of fruit added is limited). Use a vegetable wash and rinse the veggies/fruit thoroughly to rinse off any pesticide and insect residue, chop them up, and put in a blender. Make enough for the week and keep it in a container in the refrigerator and drink a cup before each meal. Get some Mason jars to take with you to work or reuse fruit juice containers to store for the week in the fridge.

Remember not to overdo fruit juices. Eating whole fruit is best with high fiber. Fiber helps you feel full and aids digestion by moving food through your intestines faster. Fiber pulls water into the digestive tract, where it helps move things along, preventing constipation.

5. **Drink lots of purified water.** Water is always the best choice of beverage for detoxifying your diet. I love the taste of plain water. Some people don't, and I understand. Not all water is created equal. Depending on where you live, tap water from the faucet often contains harmful contaminants such as metals, chlorine, fluoride, bacteria, pharmaceutical drugs, etc. If you're concerned about quality of your tap water, check your zip code's water quality on the Environmental Working Group's website. There are also ways you can have your tap water tested by sending it to a lab, order test strips or powder kits to test it for contaminants.

There are some great water filters you can install on your faucet or get yourself a water filter pitcher. Do an internet search for the best water filter pitchers to find one that filters out the most impurities possible. If you find plain water too boring, you can add some electrolyte flavoring packets to make it more exciting. Just be sure to check sugar content. Some of them sound healthy but they're not because they have lots of artificial sweeteners or sugar.

I love the Ultima Electrolyte powders when I want my water flavored a bit. Feel free to add a tablespoon of fresh fruit juice or add fresh citrus fruit, mint, or strawberries to flavor it. This is a great option for kids as well. If that's not possible, add some electrolyte powders but again, look for sugar content and flavoring that contains vitamins. Quality and moderation are key.

6. Limit coffee and soft drinks. I love my cup of morning coffee because it gives me energy to start the day (and certainly something to look forward to in the morning), but coffee is a diuretic so too much coffee can lead to dehydration. If you drink coffee, it helps to first drink 16 ounces of water after waking up. It's a great way to flush out toxins and hydrate first thing in the morning. Just know that not all coffee beans are created equal either. Some can have mold, toxins and pesticides and can be very acidic. Concerns about mold toxins have arisen among many consumers.

Select high quality coffee beans that are specialty grade and organically grown. Opt for clean, shade-grown coffee beans whenever possible. If you like to add creamer to your coffee, again be sure to read labels. Some of them are loaded with artificial ingredients that are difficult to pronounce. Choose an organic creamer with simple ingredients and keep the amount you put in your coffee to a minimum.

As for soft drinks, there's a lot of research that unequivocally shows they're bad for your health — from tooth decay to loaded sugars to artificial sweeteners and preservatives that damage the gut. It's best to eliminate them altogether. Drinking unsweetened iced tea with a tablespoon of organic fruit juice is a much better option.

7. Limit alcoholic beverages. Alcohol can be okay in small amounts. Alcohol is also a toxin, however, and should be used in moderation. New research shows that even small amounts of alcohol are damaging to the organs and the brain—not easy to hear for some, I know. I enjoy having a drink or glass of wine with dinner or a couple drinks in social situations, but just remember that the liver can only handle so much and the more toxins we burden our body with, the harder it is to rid itself of them.

If the liver isn't functioning optimally because it's overloaded with toxins (from things we can't control like the air we breathe, to the things we can control like what we eat, drink, and put ON our bodies) the liver and endocrine system gets overloaded and struggle to perform optimally. The endocrine system regulates a range of bodily functions through releasing hormones. When the endocrine system is overloaded, your glands may struggle to produce a balanced hormone level. Again, water is the best beverage for your body—it will keep you hydrated and healthy throughout the day and help you eliminate toxins. So, drink up!

8. Limit added sugars. Added sugars are found in processed foods, such as soda, packaged foods, and in sweets like granola bars, cookies, muffins, and cakes. Avoid them by choosing fresh or frozen whole fruits, rather than fruit juice, and go with natural sweeteners like honey or pure maple syrup instead of syrups containing synthetic flavoring and additives. Again, read labels and look for sugar content.

9. Individualize your diet. Your body is unique and individual. What works for you might not work the same way for others. So don't feel bad about trying new foods or changing your diet to suit your taste.

As long as you're eating healthy, nutritious, filling foods, determine what works best for your body, because everyone is different, and there's no one-size-fits-all answer to nourishing yourself.

Knowing that certain foods somehow work well together or counteract each other is helpful. If you overeat sugar, for example, your body might get rid of it by converting it to fat. And if we eat too much fat, it can slow down your body's ability to digest carbs and protein.

10. Listen to your body. Tune in to your body's hunger and fullness cues. Eat when you're genuinely hungry and stop eating when satisfied. Avoid mindless eating and practice mindful eating, focusing on taste, texture, and enjoyment of your food. This way, you will develop an awareness of how your body feels during different times of day and learn to act by these signals.

11. Consider your meal plans for the week. Some find that batch cooking meals and storing them in glass or BPA-free containers in the fridge is a great way to maintain a healthy diet throughout the week without having to cook a big meal every day. If you have children, resist the urge to make specific meals for every person in your household.

If you're the cook in the family, remember that YOU are the cook and YOU can decide how your kitchen is run. Do you want to be a short order cook? You'll run yourself ragged appealing to each person's dietary wants and creating an environment that enables family members to perpetuate bad eating habits. Making one meal for everyone is much easier to manage. Establishing boundaries around this is not easy to do if your family is accustomed to something different, but change is okay, and they will adjust.

All in all, when we ensure that our food is clean and free of harmful toxins, we're eliminating foods that don't nourish the body and replacing them with ones that do. You're also eliminating foods your body holds onto as "junk" via too much storage and inflammation.

Many toxins and harmful substances in food are unhealthy byproducts from chemical processes or fertilizers and pesticides sprayed on food or produced by cooking with oils in high quantities, like trans fats. These chemicals can be so harmful to your body that they're called "toxicants."

Choose organic produce whenever possible to avoid eating these harmful substances, especially if the produce has thin edible skin, like apples, grapes, tomatoes, etc., and be sure to always rinse produce thoroughly with clean water. Fruit and vegetable cleaners are a great investment to make your washing easier and more thorough. It will help clean off the pesticides, germs, and insect residue left in or on your produce, especially in between leafy greens.

Conventional vegetables and fruits can contain a multitude of harmful contaminants like pesticide residue and germs like salmonella and E. coli, so fruit and veggie cleaners are truly a helpful way to address this problem. You can also use relatively inexpensive distilled white vinegar to clean produce, using one part vinegar to three parts water and soaking for 10 minutes.

Avoid packaged or canned foods as much as possible; eat fresh whole fruits and vegetables instead. Conventional meats may also contain hormones and antibiotics. Research has shown that it's best to eat grass-fed meats that have fewer harmful chemicals and provide more nutrients.

So read each label carefully before you buy something and pay attention to the ingredient list. Also, try to make as much of your food as possible. Buy it fresh — don't allow it to sit for too long, follow the same guidelines for organic foods, and avoid harmful chemicals as you do with store-bought packaged foods.

Since many toxins are fat-soluble, eating lots of healthy fats with your meals will help flush them out of your system. Examples are avocados, olive oil, nuts, and seeds, coconut oil, and omega-3 fatty acids. Foods that are high in fiber are also great because they help you feel fuller and eliminate toxins better. Whole fruits, nuts, seeds, and veggies are excellent sources of fiber.

Plenty of water will also help you flush out harmful toxins. As mentioned above, water is one of your best defenses against dehydration. Drink plenty throughout the day, including a glass before each meal to improve elimination. It's extremely important to stay properly hydrated if you're doing a cleanse or detoxifying, because the toxins will come out through urine and sweat—meaning you'll be eliminating them along with excess water.

There are also herbs you can use to detoxify. Some of the best are echinacea, burdock root, dandelion root, red clover, and burdock leaf. You can freely add these to your daily diet or take them as supplements. Do so under the care of a functional medicine physician, however, because sometimes when detoxing you can feel worse before you feel better and you'll want to be under the care of a professional then.

As for your diet, start small by eliminating processed and packaged foods. You will make a good choice if you replace them with fresh fruits, veggies, and whole grains. If you're able to, make or grow as much of your food and eat organic food whenever possible. Avoid eating out as much as you can because many foods served in restaurants are also filled with chemicals, fats, and harmful ingredients you'll want to avoid.

Balancing Hormones Through Nutrition

Balancing hormones is essential for women's health and well-being. Hormones are crucial in various body functions, including reproductive health, mood regulation, metabolism, and overall physiological balance. When hormones are out of balance, women may experience a range of symptoms, such as: irregular menstrual cycles, mood swings, fatigue, weight gain, and difficulty managing stress.

While various factors can influence hormonal imbalances, nutrition is fundamental to support hormone balance. Choosing foods that support and don't overload the endocrine system is vital. Think about the endocrine system as a network of glands that secrete all hormones used by the body, like testosterone and estrogen, insulin, cortisol, and adrenaline.

Hormones act as messengers in the body, regulating various physiological processes and maintaining a delicate balance. When it is disrupted, this could cause hormonal imbalances, which can manifest in a range of symptoms and health issues.

Specific foods and plant compounds can directly influence hormone balance. For instance, phytoestrogens found in foods like flaxseed and soybeans can mimic the effects of estrogen in the body, potentially affecting hormone levels. Be careful to choose organic soy and flax. Soybeans are often genetically modified organisms (GMO). GMO soy might harbor fewer nutrients and increased herbicide residues compared to conventional or organic soy. Nevertheless, further research on the long-term health impacts of GMO soy is necessary.

Good nutrition supports the liver's detoxification process, which metabolizes and eliminates excess hormones from the body. On the other hand, poor nutrition choices can, of course, disrupt hormone balance. Excessive consumption of sugary and processed foods is likely to lead to insulin resistance, inflammation, and hormonal imbalances. Imbalances in specific nutrients, such as vitamin D, B6, magnesium, zinc, and iodine, can also affect hormone production and function.

Hormonal imbalance symptoms are dependent on which glands are not functioning optimally. Even the slightest changes can have a major impact on our bodies. When we have too much or too little of a certain hormone, whether it's insulin, cortisol, estrogen, progesterone, testosterone, or androgens, we can experience a number of undesirable symptoms.

Some symptoms of hormonal imbalances in women are listed here.

Excessive weight gain – High levels of cortisol, estrogen and insulin can contribute to belly fat.

Excessive sweating (hot flashes) – Some hormones control body temperature. Excessive sweating is a result of endocrine hormonal changes often linked to the thyroid.

Decreased sex drive – A woman's sex drive can be influenced by numerous factors, including emotional and physical well-being, past experiences, beliefs, relationships, and trauma. Illnesses, physical changes, and medications, as well as variations in estrogen and progesterone, also contribute to low libido along with health problems like diabetes or underactive thyroid.

Vaginal dryness – As we age, changes in hormone production can cause vaginal walls to thin. Thinner walls mean fewer cells that secrete moisture. This can result in vaginal dryness, causing discomfort during sexual activity, soreness, urinary tract infections (UTIs) and vaginal itching.

Extreme fatigue – Chronic (ongoing) fatigue sometimes indicates an issue with the thyroid gland or the adrenals.

Hair loss – People lose hair every day, but when losing more hair than normal it's important to get to the root cause and not just the symptoms. Hair loss in women may be associated with one or more factors, including the following:

1. A family history of female pattern hair loss, as well as hormonal changes stemming from pregnancy, childbirth, menopause, and thyroid issues.
2. Medical conditions such as scalp infections.

3. A potential side effect of specific medications, such as those prescribed for cancer, arthritis, depression, heart conditions, gout, and high blood pressure.

4. A very stressful event can cause temporary hair thinning after several months of a physical or emotional shock.

Loss of muscle mass – The truth is we lose muscle as we age. According to a Harvard study on age and muscle loss, *"On average, adults who don't strength train on a regular basis can lose four to six pounds of muscle per decade."*

Acne – A hormonal imbalance can be the culprit with acne appearing before your period. High levels of androgens and testosterone are associated with acne problems.

Digestive problems – Sex hormones affect gut flora, which alters the function of the digestive tract. Constipation, bloating, abdominal pain, or diarrhea are all possible symptoms.

If you're having any of these symptoms, make an appointment with a health care provider. A functional medicine physician can treat the whole body instead of just prescribing medications to address the symptoms. They will suggest blood tests and possibly a pelvic exam, MRI, biopsy, ultrasound and/or urine tests.

I have found it beneficial to learn from other certified professionals. I work with a functional medicine physician that has helped me more than any other medical practitioner I have seen in my life.

There are also many reputable and highly qualified practitioners you can learn from online as well. I follow Dr. Amy Shah, Dr. Josh Axe, Dr. Mark Hyman, and others for a wealth of information on their websites and social sites.

Dr. Amy Shah, who is a double-certified medical doctor and wellness expert specializing in food allergies, hormones, and gut health, states that she wishes someone would have told her in medical school that the best healers are not medications or surgery, but sun, sleep, healthy food, laughter, movement, water, fasting, good thoughts, and prayer. She says, *"There are modern tools, but you have the ultimate power to save yourself."* I couldn't agree more.

Understanding the connection between nutrition and hormone balance empowers women to take control of and make informed dietary and lifestyle choices that support their hormonal health. By adopting a balanced and nutrient-rich diet along with non-stressful exercise, women can optimize their hormone levels, alleviate symptoms of hormonal imbalance, support reproductive health, manage weight, enhance mood and energy levels, and promote overall well-being.

Journal Prompt:

Name one unhealthy eating habit per month you would like to change. What would you choose to replace it with a healthier alternative? What can you learn more about to improve your health?

4

Detoxifying Your Environment

" *I release toxins and embrace cleansing, allowing my body to rejuvenate and thrive.*

Okay, so I'm going into the next few chapters with a reminder: we are exposed to things in our environment we CANNOT control like the air we breathe outside and the electromagnetic fields (EMFs) surrounding us. However, there are things we CAN control like what we put ON and IN our bodies. These include products we use in our homes and products we can use to help filter the toxins around us. However, I want to remind you that living in constant fear is not a way to live, and we can't control everything.

I'm talking about the things we can control. Take it one day at a time. You can decide to change one thing a month to prevent overwhelm and commit to making changes slowly so it's manageable.

Here's a little-known truth: the federal government currently does not require cleaning product manufacturers to disclose the ingredients used to the public. Often, you literally can't know what's in the bottle you buy, the mister, or the spray can. These are products that you spray, wipe, and scrub with all over your home, in places where you and your family live and sleep every day.

From air fresheners to fabric softeners, from chemicals in paint to carpet, from cleaning products to the beauty products we put on our skin, we're exposed daily. If you're in a home where products containing toxic ingredients are used, potentially dangerous chemicals can make their way into your body through breathing, through the skin, and hand-to-eye or hand-to-mouth contact. This is especially true for young children who crawl and explore with their hands.

According to the Earthwise Working Group (EWG), *"Conventional cleaning product manufacturers can use almost any ingredient of their choice, and they don't have to fully disclose the formulas."*

It is crucial to prioritize what goes into your body AND to be aware of the toxins in the environment you live in. From the products you use on your body to the air you breathe in your home and the materials you interact with, detoxifying your environment plays a key role in supporting your overall well-being and minimizing potential health risks.

Environmental toxins and pollutants can have a profound impact on our health. It's important to avoid exposing yourself and your family to harmful substances especially for children, who are particularly vulnerable to hazardous chemicals that might be in everyday cleaning products. The toxins in our surroundings can influence hormonal imbalances, reproductive issues, respiratory problems, allergies, and even chronic diseases. By taking control of your environment and reducing exposure to these harmful substances, you can protect yourself and your loved ones, by supporting your health daily.

The Importance of Clean Products

The human body is naturally equipped to detoxify itself, but it can be severely compromised when subjected to toxins daily.

Add chronic stress to toxin exposure and you have a perfect storm. Just one of these alone can cause chronic inflammation in the body, but when your world is exposed to both, it can wreak havoc.

Exposure to toxic chemicals and pollutants alone over time can overload your system and can lead to long-term health complications that could interfere with the body's natural detoxification processes. These chemicals can irritate the skin, ignite skin reactions, damage hair follicles, and even cause allergic reactions such as asthma and hives.

Select products free of toxic ingredients to avoid overexposure to these harmful chemicals. By utilizing clean products, such as laundry detergents, fabric softeners, soap, shampoo, lotions, air fresheners, disinfectant sprays, and cleaning supplies free of harmful substances, you can reduce your toxins exposure while sustaining optimal health.

To detoxify your environment, use clean products daily. How do you know what toxic ingredients are lurking in your products? It's overwhelming, I know! There are resources available to us that make it easier. One of them is the Earthwise Working Group (EWG). The EWG is a non-profit organization committed to providing consumers with groundbreaking research, enabling them to make informed choices and lead a healthy life in a sustainable environment. They've created an app called the EWG Healthy Living App. You can scan products and view their ratings. Their website has a wealth of information as well.

Choosing Clean Beauty Products

The importance of clean beauty products is immense. Did you know that we absorb 60% of what we put on our bodies into our bloodstream? Think about that for a long minute. How many products do you put on your body daily between soaps, lotions, skin care, makeup, deodorants, sunscreens, and hand sanitizers? Just from your skin care alone, you may be applying six or more different products on your skin daily. Add all the different makeup products and all the other personal care products you use, and it can add up to dozens and dozens a day!

EWG asserts that, *"The EU and other countries have banned or limited more than 1,600 chemicals from personal care products. But regulators at the Food and Drug Administration in the U.S. prohibit just nine for safety reasons. Our antiquated cosmetics law needs to be updated so potentially harmful ingredients banned in other countries are no longer used in hundreds of products Americans use every day."*

Read that again, Europe has banned or limited 1600 chemicals in personal care products, whereas **the US has banned only nine!**

Do you know what is in your products? Our health is at risk every time we use a product that contains harsh chemicals and hazardous ingredients. By exploring clean alternatives free of toxic substances, you can reduce the amount of toxins you are exposed to daily and take control of your environment and health.

Clean beauty products are formulated with well-known, natural and non-toxic ingredients, minimizing the risk of harmful effects on your health. They are free from substances such as parabens, phthalates, sulfates, and synthetic fragrances, linked to various health issues: allergies, skin irritation, respiratory problems, hormone disruption and even cancer.

Clean beauty is a growing market as consumers become more aware of the dangers residing in everyday skin care and makeup. Sephora now has a clean beauty line, and many companies are shifting to meet the needs of consumers.

By implementing clean products into your life, you will contribute to overall well-being and better health. Limiting the number of toxins you are exposed to daily and being intentional about what you consume can support your body's natural detoxification process while creating a safer, cleaner environment that supports optimal health. Understanding how chemicals can impact health and taking control of your environment can create an environment where optimal health thrives.

If you're unsure about what toxin-free products to use, you can consult EWG's Healthy Living app (or www.ewg.org/skindeep), the ThinkDirty app, or Yuka app. With these databases you can search or scan beauty products and food products for ingredient safety. Lastly, Credobeauty.com has some great information on beauty products. In their "Why?" section you'll find a wealth of information along with a dirty list that is incredibly helpful.

Safe Lotions, Deodorants, Vaginal Lubricants and Sunscreens

Lotions

Check your labels and the forementioned databases and try to avoid the toxic ingredients. The majority of body lotions consist of a blend of inexpensive chemical ingredients with artificial fragrances along with filler ingredients that are petroleum-based instead of plant- based; they are even worse for the environment. Most contain paraben preservatives (propylparaben and methylparaben), PEG compounds, artificial fragrances, mineral oil, and petrolatum. Some even have a California Proposition 65 warning label warning that it could cause cancer or birth defects. Yikes!

A quick note about preservatives: any product made with water (or aloe vera), like body lotion, must have some type of preservative to give it a shelf life of more than a month or so, unless you store it in a refrigerator. This is because products containing water can develop mold, yeast, or bacteria over time. Consequently, a body lotion completely free of preservatives is not feasible.

Rather than eliminating preservatives altogether, the top clean body lotion brands typically incorporate a minimal amount of a safer preservative that remains effective in preventing microbial growth in their products. If you prefer to avoid preservatives entirely, consider opting for a body oil or skin balm that lacks water in its formulation.

Antiperspirants and Deodorants

Aluminum antiperspirant vs. natural deodorant: aluminum-based antiperspirants work by blocking sweat pores. There is some controversy around the safety of aluminum in antiperspirants that is still being researched, so I choose to steer clear of them.

In contrast, the majority of natural deodorants utilize ingredients such as baking soda, arrowroot powder, clay, or charcoal to absorb moisture. Instead of preventing sweat, these ingredients assist in absorbing sweat and neutralizing or masking odor. Compared to products employing metals to block sweat pores, they may not be as effective in absorbing sweat for some individuals. However, those of us who choose natural deodorants do so because we've decided to use a gentler product with as few chemicals as possible.

Natural ingredients, however, can also cause skin irritation, such as deodorants with high amounts of baking soda, as can other ingredients in natural deodorants. The first time I tried a natural deodorant, my armpits broke out it a horrible itchy rash, apparently due to my sensitivity to large amounts of baking soda. I had to switch my natural deodorant to the sensitive version that uses arrowroot powder, and it works beautifully for me. There are many out there, but my personal favorite is from Native in Coconut Vanilla scent.

Nearly everyone will have to undergo some trial and error to determine which natural deodorant ingredients suit them best, along with finding the right scent, if any, that complements their individual chemistry. Moreover, there's the aspect of application, as natural deodorants come in various forms such as sprays, powders, putties, creams, gels, sticks, and more. A valuable tip, applicable to most natural deodorants, is to hold the product under your armpit for a few seconds to allow it to warm and soften before swiping.

Look for deodorants that are free from:

- Parabens
- Fragrance
- Triclosan
- Phthalates
- Proplyene glycol (in some cases)
- Polyethylene glycol (PEG)
- TEA and DEA
- Aluminum

Vaginal Lubricants

Did you know that commercial lubricants can affect your vaginal wall health and cause infection? If you are one of the many women experiencing vaginal dryness causing irritation and/or vaginal infections, pay close attention here. Vaginal dryness, for instance, can happen to women of any age, due to the side-effects of medication or treatment, beauty products (soaps, perfumes, douching, bubble baths, detergents) that can disrupt the pH balance in the vagina, and hormone-disrupting exposures (smoking, eating foods that are hormone disrupters, or exposure to toxins). As we age, the vaginal wall lining becomes thinner and is more prone to irritation.

Dr. Sara Celik, ND cautions that the chemicals and ingredients in some vaginal lubricants may disrupt healthy vaginal flora and can act as endocrine disrupters that interfere with your hormones. These disruptions can not only cause irritation but also cancerous tumors, birth defects, and fertility issues. She cites one study that showed vaginal lubricants were associated with more than a threefold greater risk of acquiring a sexually transmitted infection (STI). She advises women to switch from commercial lubricants to natural lubes because many commercial lubricants can create a breeding ground for yeast and other pathogens (microorganisms that cause infections). She advises choosing something non-toxic and organic, such as coconut oil, olive oil, plain aloe vera or a non-toxic lubricant free of harmful chemicals and ingredients.

Some lubricants like coconut oil and olive oil are NOT safe to use with condoms, however. Do your research and/or consult your gynecologist and remember that chemicals and toxic ingredients that go on your skin also go into your body. This means it's up to you to protect your female parts and choose non-toxic products.

If you prefer a store-bought lubricant, use one that has been reviewed by the EWG, Yuka, or ThinkDirty. My personal favorite lubricant product not in my kitchen that's also safe to use with toys and condoms is Shine Organic naturally hydrating, aloe-and-water-based personal lubricant by Maude. It's not cheap but neither is my vagina!

Clean Sunscreens

Oh, the sun! It's the lifeforce of our world. Getting sunlight is essential for life with numerous health benefits. *Medical News Today* contends that getting sunlight is an important source of Vitamin D. You can either get vitamin D from your diet and supplements, but sunlight is an important source and supports healthy bones, manages calcium levels, reduces inflammation, and supports the immune system and glucose metabolism. However, there is great awareness to be cautious about spending too much time in the sun, as too much exposure to UV radiation from the sun can cause skin cancer. As in all things, moderation is key.

Medical News Today also affirms that finding the balance can enable individuals to sustain optimal vitamin D levels and experience the mental health benefits of a sunny day without exposing themselves to undue risks. SPF (sun protection factor) measures how long a sunscreen will protect you from ultraviolet light (UV) rays. SPF works by prolonging your skin's natural defenses against the sun. The sun emits two primary types of radiation: UVA and UVB rays. UVA rays are responsible for aging skin, leading to wrinkles and sagging.

UVB rays are more carcinogenic and often responsible for sunburn. UVA rays also make UVB rays more reactive, so combined the two can be deadly if too much time is spent in the sun. Choose a sunscreen with broad-spectrum UV protection that will block both UVA and UVB rays. An SPF of 30 provides 30 times more protection than your normal skin without sunscreen.

For example, if you normally burn after being in the sun for 10 minutes, using a SPF of 30 gives you 5 hours (10 x 30 = 300 minutes or five hours) of sun time without burning. However, sweat and swimming will reduce that time, so reapplying is necessary.

However, many sunscreens contain chemicals that are not only toxic to the body that can negatively affect your hormonal system but are also toxic to the environment, ocean life, and coral reefs. In 2021, Hawaii passed a bill prohibiting sunscreens that contain chemicals known to contribute to the degradation of the state's coral reefs and other marine life. Oxybenzone and octinoxate, used in more than 3,500 of the world's most popular sunscreen products, are now prohibited.

As far back as 2008, EWG urged the FDA to investigate the safety of oxybenzone, pointing to substantial evidence suggesting its easy skin penetration and potential disruption of the hormone system. By 2020, four studies supported the FDA's conclusion that oxybenzone can function as an endocrine disruptor, heightening the risk of breast cancer and endometriosis.

Oxybenzone is found in human breast milk, amniotic fluid, urine, and blood. Children may be more susceptible than adults to harm from this ingredient due to its *"potential for higher absorption and bioaccumulation"* – this is according to the FDA.

EWG also suggests that consumers avoid spray sunscreens. These products pose various concerns, including potential ingredient toxicity, contamination issues, and inhalation hazards. One particularly alarming issue is the identification of benzene in spray sunscreens, a known carcinogen. This contamination led to recalls of many aerosol products in 2021, 2022 and 2023. I know, I know—applying sunscreen to a squirming child is MUCH easier using a spray but consider applying sunscreen before leaving the house so your child isn't trying to run from you when they're ready to play outside. If you prefer a spray sunscreen, choose one with a good rating from EWG.

I cringe when I see a parent spray toxic sunscreen on children's faces at the beach or pool right before they go in the water. Not only are they breathing in the toxic fumes, they're also getting it in their eyes! Be aware of this the next time you put sunscreen on yourself, your child, or loved ones.

You may be wondering which sunscreens are reliably safe to use. It can be truly daunting to discern which brands to trust and navigate the selection of a healthy sunscreen. For this reason, I recommend using EWG's annual guide to sunscreens. You can find it at www.ewg.org/sunscreen.

They recommend a comprehensive approach to sun safety, including sun-safe practices like wearing hats, sunglasses and avoiding the sun during peak hours.

Choosing Natural Household Cleaners

You can boost your health and preserve your well-being by utilizing natural cleaning products. Many cleaning products can contain harmful ingredients that may interfere with your hormonal system. When choosing products for your home, opt to utilize environmentally friendly cleaners free of harmful chemicals and substances that may have negative effects. To clear your home of toxic substances, look for environmentally friendly household cleansers free of pesticides and dangerous chemicals.

When selecting home cleaning products, buy cleaners free of harmful chemicals and substances such as bleach, chlorine, chlorine derivatives, mineral spirits, synthetic fragrances, and preservatives. Instead of worrying about whether the cleaning product is toxic, look for environmentally friendly cleaners, or make your own. There are many great recipes for homemade cleaning recipes online and on Pinterest. With store-bought cleaners, be careful of marketing a "natural" product that isn't natural. There are many claims about "naturalness," which doesn't mean there are no toxic ingredients. That's why the Environmental Working Group (EWG), has created a database of more than 2,000 household cleaners. I find the list helpful for selecting environmentally friendly and hypoallergenic cleaning products. To view a list of products rated for toxicity go to www.ewg.org.

Creating a Toxin-Free Home

Unfortunately, home is one of the most significant places where toxins are released into the atmosphere to be absorbed through skin and mucous membranes. Surprisingly, the inside of our home can be more toxic than outside air. According to Madesafe.org, claims like all natural, green, and clean, do not have standard legal or regulatory definitions. Know the ingredients in your home cleaning products and eliminate toxic substances from your home. Finally, carefully choose eco-friendly candles and air fresheners free of synthetic fragrances to keep the air in your home clean and safe.

By taking proactive measures to eliminate toxins and reduce exposure to hazardous chemicals, you can create a space that supports your health and contributes to a better quality of life. In addition to supporting your body's natural detoxification process, you can create an environment that encourages wellness and helps mitigate side effects caused by products in your home. Deciding to make a clean and toxin-free living space might sound daunting at first, but it's simple once you know what to look out for.

Steps to Create a Toxin-Free Home

1.   **Identify possible toxins in your home.** Before making significant changes to eliminate toxins from your home, identify the substances that represent health risks to you or your family. For example, if someone in the family suffers from allergies or asthma, look for potential culprits such as pet dander or dust mites. Replace carpet with wood flooring if possible, especially in bedrooms and living rooms (where we spend the most time). Below is a chart listing common household volatile organic compounds to be aware of.

Household sources of VOC's:

Building Materials	Home & Personal Care Products	Human Activities
Paints	Air fresheners	Smoking
Varnishes	Fragrance-scented	Dry cleaning
Caulks	candles	Photocopiers
Adhesives	Cleaning products	Cooking
Carpet & vinyl flooring	Cosmetics	Buring wood in any
Composit wood products	Fuel oil & gasoline	capacity where you
Upholstery & foam	(both when used or stored)	inhale the fumes

Shockingly, carpet is highly impregnated with chemicals, some potentially harmful to human health. On the other hand, wood flooring is an excellent alternative to carpet and is naturally anti-bacterial, anti-fungal, and anti-microbial. It will not cause allergies or asthma triggers such as dust mites. Wood floors can also be easily treated by natural solutions such as the well-known washing with soap and water or treating them occasionally with essential oils.

I have carpet in my home and my husband isn't eager to replace it, but I try to keep windows open to bring in fresh air and we use an air purifier in our home.

**2.	Choose eco-friendly cleaners for your home.** Look for products free of harsh chemicals, such as chlorine and synthetic fragrances, which may cause health problems such as nausea, sore throat, headache, or dizziness. Harsh chemicals can also negatively affect the health of pets.

A friend of mine couldn't figure out why her cat kept throwing up beyond the normal hairball. She found that the floor cleaner her housecleaner used was severely toxic to her cat. Once she started using a safer product, the excessive vomiting stopped.

By implementing green cleaning products, you support your body's natural detoxification process while creating a cleaner home. Be sure to read the labels on household cleaners carefully and select cleansers free of toxic ingredients. Consider making your own cleaning products using baking soda with water or vinegar along with essential oils (such as lavender, peppermint, rosemary, cedarwood) or herbal teas (chamomile). Use the trusty ewg.org website to find other non-toxic products.

3. Create a natural cleaning routine. Regularly cleaning areas that cause unpleasant odors (toilets, sinks, appliances, and pet areas) you can prevent odors before they ever start.

4. Open the windows. Open windows regularly to improve ventilation and circulate fresh air. Use air purifiers that come with HEPA filters to remove airborne pollutants and allergens.

5. Practice safe scents. Avoid smoking indoors and limit the usage of harsh chemical-based air fresheners. This may be tough to hear but removing air fresheners and other fragrances and toxic candles will be safer for you and your family. Burning candles is a simple way to alter the atmosphere and awaken the senses through fragrance and visual appeal. Despite their potential to enhance your rituals, it's essential to acknowledge that candles may have adverse effects on your health. Opt for candles with a 100% cotton wick whenever feasible, or explore options with a wick made of wood and clean-burning soy wax or beeswax. Ensure the labels explicitly state "100%", and choose wax that is naturally derived or sustainably sourced. Some candles may be labeled as "beeswax" while still being a blend of paraffin and another wax, so carefully read labels or contact the brand for clarification if needed.

When cleaning, realize that toxic chemicals can quickly enter the air. Consider making your own cleansers for spills and stains. Instead of using store-bought air fresheners, opt for homemade essential oil room sprays, use an essential oil diffuser or simmer pots with citrus peels, herbs and/or spices.

6. Surround yourself with greenery. Many plants are great for filtering the air. The spider plant, peace lily, snake plant and golden pathos are a few that improve indoor air quality since they naturally filter the air. (If you have children or pets, make sure to check for toxicity warnings if ingested.)

7. Install a water filtration system to remove impurities and contaminants from your tap water. This ensures access to clean and safe drinking water, free from toxins such as chlorine, lead, and other pollutants. Also, have your water tested regularly to ensure it's free of contaminants and impurities. If you'd like to check the quality of your drinking water, search your zip code on EWG's tap water database at www.ewg.org/tapwater.

8. Non-toxic cookware and food storage. Choose cookware made from safe materials like stainless steel, cast iron, glass, or ceramic. Avoid non-stick coatings that may contain perfluorochemicals (PFCs). Use glass or stainless-steel containers for food storage instead of plastic containers that may leach harmful chemicals into your food.

9. Avoid chemicals and synthetic fragrances in personal care products and cosmetics. Look for products that are free of parabens, phthalates, triclosan, and other potentially harmful ingredients. Also, look for package labeling for potentially hazardous substances, such as dyes or synthetic fragrances. Check out the "Why Clean?" area on the credobeauty.com website and search EWG's Skin Deep®

database and Guide to Sunscreens for the most up-to-date information. Yuka is also a great app that deciphers product labels and analyzes the health impact of food products and cosmetics.

10. Check areas in your home for high Electromagnetic Fields (EMFs).   EMF's are generated by various electronic devices and technologies, and while the scientific community is still studying potential health effects, some individuals may choose to take precautions. Here are some general suggestions on how individuals can reduce their exposure to EMFs.

1. Maintain a safe distance from electronic devices. For example, use speakerphone or a wired headset instead of holding your cellphone to your ear.

2. Use Airplane Mode: When not actively using your cellphone, switch it to airplane mode to reduce EMF exposure. This cuts off wireless communication functions.

3. Limit Wireless Device Usage: Reduce the time spent using wireless devices, such as laptops, tablets, and smartphones. Opt for wired connections whenever possible.

4. Use EMF Protection Products. Some individuals use products like EMF shielding materials, cell phone cases, or clothing designed to reduce exposure. There are even testing

devices you can use to test the amount of EMF's in your home. However, the efficacy of such products is a topic of debate, and it's essential to research and choose reputable options.

Journal Prompt:

What is ONE new thing you can do PER MONTH to minimize your exposure to toxins?

Take baby steps that won't seem daunting to change everything all at once. By changing one aspect per month, by the end of the year, you will have 12 different areas of your environment free of harmful toxins.

5

Movement and Exercise

" *Through movement, I am attuned to my physical needs, nurturing my health and well-being with each conscious motion.*

Physical activity is an essential part of your journey integral to achieving the ultimate goal of wellness. Moving your body daily will get your blood pumping and bring oxygen to your vessels and arteries. Better circulation means lower blood pressure, tension, anxiety, stress, and also reduces the chances of succumbing to heart disease, the biggest killer of all. Regular exercise also can help reduce pain and discomfort.

Exercise is crucial to any wellness plan. It is one of the ways we show love and care to our bodies, promote optimal levels of flexibility and strength, and keep metabolism functioning at an optimal level. This is most effective as part of your daily routine. Commit to scheduling time in your day to just do it.

Consulting with a fitness professional or a certified instructor can provide guidance on proper body movement and specific techniques and exercises designed to your specific needs and goals.

The Benefits of Regular Movement

There have certainly been times in my life that I neglected movement. I found it overwhelming trying to fit exercise into my day, but I paid the price. In my early thirties I noticed that my energy and patience waned, while my midsection continued to grow into a belly pooch that looked like I was perpetually pregnant. Someone even asked me when I was expecting! I was mortified and so was she! Looking back, it's kind of funny, but I realized I was overworking myself and rarely incorporated self-care into my routine other than an occasional massage.

I was trying to build my sales career but sacrificed my health at the same time. My adrenals were completely shot, my periods were brutally painful with cramps, headaches, neckaches, and extreme fatigue, and I was beginning to experience debilitating morning joint pain.

What I discovered is that as we age, we find that the same workouts we did when we were younger are no longer giving the results, we seek now. This is often due to changing hormones. Physically overworking the body can overstress, causing increased cortisol production, negating some of the positive effects of regular exercise. For this reason, experts now find that regular movement that calms the nervous system but gets your blood pumping is most effective.

As women, we face unique challenges throughout our lives. We have a higher risk of low bone mass and osteoporosis and go through unique hormonal changes at different points in life. So, let's move it ladies! Find a way to move that you love and make it a new healthy habit.

Benefits of movement for women:

- Digestive health
- Weight loss
- Cardiovascular conditioning
- Flexibility and coordination
- Improved mental health
- Increased energy levels
- Improved mood and sleep
- Protects against injury and disease
- Helps prevent and manage stress
- Supports longevity
- Hormonal balance
- Stronger bones

Exercises for Women's Health

Following are exercises that keep the body healthy:

Types of Exercise

Flexibility Exercises
Stretching reduces your risk of injury during other activities. Gently stretch for 10 minutes before any workout.

Ideas:
- Yoga
- Pilates

Aerobic Exercise
Aerobic exercise will increase heart rate, work muscles, build endurance and increase breathing rate. Experts recommend at least 30 minutes a day 5 days a week.

Ideas:
- Take a brisk walk
- Go dancing
- Sign up for an aerobics class
- Swim
- Ride a bike
- Play Tennis

Anaerobic Exercises
Anaerobic exercises include brief, strength-based activities.

Ideas:
- Sprinting
- Jumping
- Strength Training

Strength Training
Strength training helps build strong bones and muscles. More muscles means you burn more calories, even at rest. It is recommended to be done 2-3 times a week. Be careful however, don't lift too heavy or go to fast. Pay close attention to form.

Ideas
- Join a strength training class
- Use weights, elastic bands, or plastic tubes
- lift weights at home or just any objects on hand
- Try calisthenics such as push-ups, squats, and sit-ups

Walking: An excellent way for women to exercise. Many women already walk daily but don't get enough aerobic exercise to promote health. Aim for at least 7,000 steps a day. Walking is easy and can be done almost anywhere. You can also add an incline or stairs to your walking routine to boost the intensity level of your workouts. I have found beautiful spots in my neighborhood with lots of stairs I can climb to increase my heart rate. If you love nature, as I do, and the weather is permitting, walking outdoors in nature is beneficial for body and mind. I like to walk and work my upper body at the same time. I do this by holding my arms out like a bird and using my upper back muscles pull my arms back and forth like I'm flapping my arms. Squeeze as you pull back and it works out the upper back nicely. Same thing with bicep curls while walking. Slowly flex your muscles while doing bicep curls. I do 20 reps 3 times each while walking and I can definitely see a difference in my muscle definition.

Swimming: Works your entire body, it's a great way to increase your heart rate, tone muscles, and build strength and endurance. It's a great option for those with injuries since it's easy on the joints.

Lifting Weights: Essential for women to develop lean muscle tissue and promote bone health. You don't have to lift heavy weights to see results. Women who lift regularly see results after three months.

Core Strength: Strengthening core muscles is essential for women to keep the body healthy and reduce risk of back injury and muscle strain. Exercises such as Pilates and yoga improve flexibility, balance, and strengthen core muscles. Yoga exercises can be done anywhere without equipment, while Pilates is done in a studio with special equipment such as exercise balls, mats, and springs. Both activities are great because they improve balance and build core strength to help prevent falls.

Pelvic Floor Exercises: Essential for women, pelvic floor exercises help seniors gain control of bowels and bladder. Working the pelvic floor helps prevent incontinence and urinary tract problems in later life.

Cardiovascular Training: As a women age, they may notice waning stamina. Cardiovascular exercises are the best way to strengthen the heart and get blood pumping oxygen. Cycling, running, stair climbing, jump roping, and using the elliptical are a few great cardio exercises. Twenty minutes a day makes a visible difference.

Pilates: Pilates is an excellent way to improve flexibility and balance to strengthen core muscles. Many gyms have special equipment that can be used for Pilates exercises, or you can buy a Pilates DVD (if you still have a DVD player) or find online videos on YouTube or Instagram. These exercises are great to improve balance and prevent falls.

High-Intensity Interval Training (HIIT): HIIT workouts involve alternating periods of intense exercise with very brief recovery periods. This training can be highly effective in improving cardiovascular fitness, burning calories, and boosting metabolism. HIIT workouts include exercises like burpees, jumping jacks, mountain climbers, and high knees. Start with short intervals and gradually increase the intensity as your fitness level improves.

Rowing: Oars are excellent for women because they help keep the heart healthy, strengthen arm and core muscles, and promote hormone balance. You don't need oars to start rowing; you can sit on a chair and hold the paddler in your hand. You'll see how this exercise improves your balance within a few sessions.

Just don't overdo it. Utilizing a trainer can help with form to address issues related to your unique body. Remember to feel how your body reacts, start at an appropriate fitness level, and slowly increase intensity and duration as you progress.

If you're taking any kind of high intensity or strength conditioning classes, don't be competitive with others in the class. It's more important to keep your form on point to avoid injury. I injured my shoulder in a CrossFit class and I've seen friends and colleagues do the same.

So, slow it down, breathe, keep your form, and don't try to prove how much you can lift. Lift enough to provide resistance and go slowly. That way you can do fewer reps and you're still building muscle.

Here are some tips to help incorporate exercise into your daily routine:

1. Choose your workout space
2. Put on your gym clothes
3. Don't worry about equipment if working out at home
4. Use your devices to get new workouts
5. Set realistic fitness goals
6. Keep track of your progress

Make your workout fun, not something you dread. You can incorporate workout routines like squats into activities like gardening, or calf raises while cooking. Whatever the case, find something that makes exercise simple and fun, wearing headphones to listen to music so it won't feel like it's a dreaded chore.

Many applications can help you keep track of your exercise routine. You can also use apps for motivation because they remind you to exercise daily and set goals and track your progress. There are many out there. YouTube has great workouts. Fitcoach is a great app I enjoy using.

Keeping tabs on your progress is beneficial as it allows you to assess whether your efforts are yielding positive results. You can do this by jotting down your exercises, recording how much weight you lift, and checking your body fat percentage to see if it's going down.

Just don't give up. The key to staying consistent is to make exercise less complicated by choosing fun activities you enjoy. Spending time in nature is a great way to move and ground yourself. Seeing the beauty around you is a reminder that you're not alone.

Grounding the body, often referred to as "grounding" or "earthing," involves connecting your body directly to the earth by walking barefoot on natural surfaces, sitting, or lying on the ground, or using grounding devices. Many people believe that grounding has several potential benefits.

There are shoes designed specifically for grounding, often referred to as "grounding" shoes or "earthing" shoes. These are made with materials that allow electrical conductivity, enabling a connection with the Earth while wearing them. The soles of grounding shoes typically contain conductive materials, such as carbon or metal that have a conductive pathway allowing the flow of electrons between your feet and the ground. I bought myself a pair of Xero shoes and love them for my nature walks.

Create a music playlist to feel empowered while you exercise. You can find a playlist that motivates you. I love *"Queen B's Girl Power Mix,"* or *"Girl Power Workout"* on Spotify, but find a mix or create your own that motivates you to move and de-stress.

A good rule of thumb when designing an exercise program is to follow the "talk test." This is a simple method used during exercise to gauge the intensity of physical activity based on your ability to speak comfortably while exerting effort. It can be a handy tool to assess whether you're exercising at an appropriate intensity level for your goals. For example, if your goal is to just move it or relieve stress for hormone balance, it's great to begin with light intensity workouts.

Here's how the talk test works:

1.   **Light intensity:** During light-intensity exercise, such as a leisurely walk or gentle yoga, you should be able to speak comfortably, hold a conversation, and not feel breathless or overly exerted.

2.   **Moderate intensity:** During moderate-intensity exercise, such as a brisk walk or steady-paced cycling, you should still be able to speak, but your breathing may become quicker, and you may need to take occasional pauses in your speech to catch your breath. You should feel challenged but still able to hold a conversation.

3.   **Vigorous intensity:** During vigorous-intensity exercise, such as high-intensity interval training (HIIT) or sprinting, you will find it difficult to speak in full sentences. Your breathing will be rapid, and you may only be able to say a few words at a time. You will feel significantly exerted and may need to focus more on your breathing than on talking.

By paying attention to your ability to speak comfortably during exercise, you can adjust the intensity level to match your goals. If you're aiming for a light-to-moderate intensity workout, you should be able to converse easily. If you're aiming for a more intense workout, you should find it challenging to speak in full sentences.

It's important to note that the talk test is a subjective measure and may vary depending on individual fitness levels, age, and health conditions. It serves as a general guideline rather than a precise measurement of exercise intensity. Other methods, such as heart rate monitoring or rating perceived exertion (RPE), can be used in conjunction with the talk test to provide a more comprehensive assessment of exercise intensity.

Yoga for Women's Wellness

Yoga is an ancient practice that originated 5,000 years ago in India, to bring about spiritual enlightenment. While it provides many benefits besides spiritual culture, through its harmonious combination of movement, breath, and mindfulness, yoga cultivates flexibility and strength in mind, body and spirit.

The Power of Yoga

Yoga encompasses many physical postures known as asanas (with given English translations) combined with regulated breathing. While there are many kinds of yoga, Hatha yoga is the most popular. A harmonized combination of physical poses and controlled breathing techniques form the foundation of most yoga forms today. Yoga can even be practiced during pregnancy. However, learning the basic poses and improvising depends on your needs.

Starting something new can be intimidating but yoga is a practice that is not only exercise, but it can also be emotionally and mentally transformative. Originating as a spiritual practice, yoga has gained popularity for its role in fostering both physical and mental well-being. As of 2017, according to the National Center for Complementary and Integrative health, more than 21 million adults in the United States are practicing yoga. Many different types of yoga are being created to cater to different philosophies. The types of yoga described below are the foundation for most classes available these days. Their descriptions will give you the basic knowledge to select classes. One thing to keep in mind is that yoga is an eight-limbed path to enlightenment defined by Patanjali's *"Yoga Sutra."* Asanas (poses) are the physical practices we call yoga and is just one limb of that path. This is the reason why yoga classes often incorporate pranayama (breathing exercises), meditation, and other philosophies. They help introduce the practitioner to more than one limb of yoga. When first starting yoga, you'll likely be introduced to a couple of its limbs: the asanas (poses) and pranayama (mindful breathing). The eight-limbed path of yoga is as follows:

The 8 Limb Path

These are some of the most common types of yoga:

1.   **Hatha yoga:** Hatha is a gentle foundational style of yoga emphasizing physical postures and alignment. It's a great choice for beginners and serves as the basis for many other yoga styles.

2.   **Vinyasa yoga:** My personal favorite, vinyasa is a dynamic flowing style of yoga that links breath with

movement. It often involves a series of poses creating continuous flow.

3.   **Ashtanga yoga:** Ashtanga is a vigorous physically demanding form of yoga that follows a specific sequence of postures similar to Vinyasa, but with a more structured approach.

4.   **Bikram yoga:** Bikram yoga (also known as "hot yoga") is practiced in a room heated to high temperatures. It comprises a set series of 26 postures and 2 breathing exercises.

5.   **Iyengar yoga:** Iyengar yoga places strong emphasis on precise alignment and the use of props (such as belts and blocks) to help students perform poses with great accuracy.

6.   **Kundalini yoga:** Kundalini yoga combines postures, breathing techniques, and meditation with the aim to awake the dormant energy at the base of the spine, known as kundalini.

7.   **Yin yoga:** Yin yoga is a slow-paced style, focusing on holding poses for an extended period (often three to five minutes) to stretch and target connective tissues.

8.   **Restorative yoga:** Restorative yoga is all about relaxation and stress relief. It uses props for supporting the body in passive poses, allowing for deep relaxation.

These are just a few of the many yoga styles. The choice of yoga style depends on individual preferences, physical abilities, and the goals you want to achieve through your practice.

The benefits you get from practicing yoga regularly are vast. Here are just a handful:

BENEFITS OF YOGA FOR YOUR HEALTH

Yoga makes you feel good

Yoga boosts the immune system

Yoga increases body flexibility

Yoga helps you to focus on one thing

Yoga increases strength in the body

Yoga reduces excess anxiety

Developing a Personal Yoga Practice

Yoga can be done at home or in a group setting in a studio. There are many benefits to practicing yoga alone or with others. If you enjoy class settings, find a yoga studio you love near you. If you prefer working out at home, all you need is a yoga mat and a good video. You can find some great apps and videos online. I love the Asana Rebel app, as well as Yoga with Adrien and Yoga with Kassandra on YouTube. The online Hips Like Honey series by Manuela Mitevova is also fantastic if you have hip pain. There are so many resources for good yoga classes. You can find them by simply searching online. I follow Manuela and Kassandra on Instagram and always appreciate their wisdom.

I recently took a *Yoga with Kassandra* online class called *"Water Element Vin to Yin Hip Opening Emotions Yoga,"* and its hands down one of my favorites! She shares that each element has something to teach us, a gift to offer, and wisdom to take into your life. The element of water is all about fluidity and linked to your hips and sacral chakra, and the ability to go with the flow explore the depths of your being.

Kassandra wisely points out that when water is still and stagnant it becomes murky and swamp-like, but when you allow water to flow, you have beautiful streams and clear water. She affirms that you can translate this to how you deal with your own emotions. When you suppress, control, or repress them, things get murky and stuck, but when you allow your emotions to run through you, that's when you begin to get clarity. Her vin-to-yin yoga class features fluid movements that move at a slower pace focusing on holding poses for longer periods of time. I find that nearly every time I take one of her online classes I leave with a new piece of wisdom.

Yoga is a spiritual transformative practice allowing you to find inner peace. It is also essential to know that yoga is not a quick fix. It's not difficult, but I find that consistency and patience is key to seeing and feeling results. Here are some steps to help you establish a personal yoga practice.

1. Set up a space for yourself to practice. This can be a place in your house, like the living room or bedroom area, or somewhere outdoors like a park bench or backyard. I love doing yoga poses after a walk or climbing stairs at the local park near my home. At the end of my walk, I do some yoga poses on the grass to finish off my workout while the trees sway in the breeze. It feels amazing! If you practice at home, ensure you have enough space to do so safely and comfortably. The last thing you want to do is injure yourself, so find a quiet place where you will not be disturbed.

2. Choose comfortable clothing. You can wear what you feel most comfortable wearing and allows you to move freely.

3. Prepare your mat. If you don't have a yoga mat, you can purchase one online or at the store. There are many types of yoga mats, thick and thin ones. When you first begin your practice, you might find that a thicker mat gives you added cushion and comfort. As your practice grows and becomes more advanced, a thin mat may be better for you because it can help improve your balance.

4. Start with a warm-up. Most yoga classes incorporate a warm-up, but if not make sure you warm up beforehand to avoid injury. You can do this by walking around, doing squats, jump squats, jumping jacks, or doing a few simple poses. To warm up even further, you can incorporate basic yoga poses such as the Warrior I or II pose or the Downward Facing Dog pose to help loosen your muscles.

5. Locate and listen to your breath. Breath is an excellent tool for meditation and yoga in general. Taking control of your breath is important in yoga because deep breathing helps the body relax more than shallow breathing allows. Beginning yoga poses such as the Sun Salutation or Warrior I or II poses can be used to practice your breathing and let your heart rate go down.

6. Stay focused and aware of what you're doing. When practicing yoga, try to avoid focusing on other thoughts and things around you. This can be done by focusing on things like counting each breath, listening to meditative style music, or reminding yourself how relaxed you feel after your practice.

7. End your yoga session with relaxation. At the end of each session, take a few minutes to relax after practicing. You can use simple poses such as the Downward Facing Dog to relax your body and mind. You can also sit in a chair or table, meditate, or hang out with a friend for 15-20 minutes after practice.

Breathing Techniques

Yoga breathing techniques, often referred to as pranayama, offer a profound pathway to cultivate mindfulness, enhance physical well-being, and establish a deeper connection between body and mind. These techniques involve conscious control of your breath, harnessing its power to influence the nervous system, reduce stress, and promote relaxation. From the rhythmic and calming Ujjayi breath to the invigorating Kapalabhati, each technique carries unique benefits. Deepening breath awareness through pranayama amplifies the benefits of yoga postures, enhancing the flow of oxygen, vital energy, and harmony throughout the body.

Whether seeking tranquility or revitalization, the practice of yoga breathing techniques fosters equilibrium within, fostering a sense of balance, presence, and overall well-being.

Try the following common yoga breathing techniques (pranayama) to see how they make you feel:

1.   **Ujjayi Breath (Ocean Breath):** This technique involves breathing through the nose with a slightly constricted throat, creating a gentle, audible sound resembling ocean waves. It helps calm the mind, regulate breath, and enhance focus during yoga asanas.

2.   **Deep Belly Breathing (diaphragmatic breathing):** Inhale deeply through your nose, allowing your abdomen to fully expand. Exhale completely, gently contracting your abdomen. This technique promotes relaxation, reduces stress, and enhances lung capacity.

3.   **Kapalabhati (Skull Shining Breath):** This is an energizing breath technique involving rapid, forceful exhalations through the nose, followed by passive inhalation. It helps clear the respiratory system, increase oxygen intake, and invigorate the body.

4. Nadi Shodhana (alternate nostril breathing): Using your thumb and ring finger, alternate blocking one nostril while inhaling and exhaling through the other. This technique balances the left and right hemispheres of the brain, promoting mental clarity and harmony.

5. Bhramari (Bee Breath): Inhale deeply and exhale making a humming sound like a bee. This technique has a calming effect, reducing anxiety and stress. It also helps to soothe the nervous system.

6. Sheetali/Sitali (Cooling Breath): Roll your tongue into a tube or purse your lips and inhale deeply through the mouth. Exhale through the nose. This breath cools the body and calms the mind, making it particularly useful during hot weather or moments of agitation.

7. Bhastrika (Bellows Breath): This is a rapid, forceful breath where you inhale and exhale vigorously through the nose. It increases oxygen supply, invigorates the body, and generates warmth. It's often used to energize and activate the respiratory system.

8. Anulom Vilom (alternate nostril breathing with retention): Inhale through one nostril while blocking the other with your thumb, then exhale through the opposite nostril. This technique balances energy channels, calms the mind, and enhances focus.

9.   **Box Breathing:** Inhale slowly for a count of four, then hold your breath for a count of four, exhale for a count of four, then hold the breath for another count of four. This technique promotes balance and relaxation.

Remember that each of these techniques serves a specific purpose - choose the one that aligns with your current needs and goals. Incorporate these pranayama techniques into your yoga practice, starting with a few minutes and gradually increasing the duration as you become more comfortable. If you're new to pranayama, consider learning from a qualified yoga instructor to ensure you're practicing safely and effectively.

Journal Prompt:

Describe your ideal movement practice. How do you feel after doing this exercise? How can you create a realistic plan to engage in it regularly? Is there any part of your body that feels unusually tight, tense, or sore? What feelings arise from this discomfort? Do you find that certain yoga poses or breathing techniques release tension, even if it's temporary?

6

Meditation and Mindfulness

" *I cultivate mindfulness, grounding myself in the present moment and nurturing my inner peace.*

When you're mindful, you're aware of thoughts and emotions you're currently experiencing. You also recognize that thoughts and emotions aren't good or bad, but simply experiences.

Meditating is a way for a person to become more mindful. When meditate, turn your attention inward to become more aware of your thoughts and emotions. This allows negative thoughts and feelings to pass in and out of your mind without becoming too attached to them.

For example, if you feel a negative thought like, "I keep making the wrong decisions," reframe it to, "I may not always make perfect decisions, but I am learning and gaining wisdom with each choice. I trust myself to make better decisions in the future." Or if you think, "I can't do this, it's too difficult," instead reframe it into, "This is a challenging task, but I can break it down into smaller steps. With persistence and effort, I can make progress." Being mindful helps to recognize these thought patterns without letting them to overtake your emotions. This allows you to develop a healthier outlook on life.

Mindfulness is a way to calm the mind and to focus internally and less on the outside world. When your mind is focused on external thoughts, you worry about things that may or may not happen. This can cause anxiety; however, when you focus on internal thoughts, you're more aware of your body. You can mindfully choose what you want to focus on, positive or negative.

7 BENEFITS OF
Meditation

 ## Reduces stress and anxiety
Meditating daily has been shown in clinical research to be a useful aid in the reduction of chronic anxiety and anxiety disorders.

 ## Strengthens the immune system
Mindfulness meditation has shown increases in electrical activity in specific parts of the brain. When stimulated, the immune system brain-function regions work more effectively.

 ## Improves sleep quality
Regular meditation encourages the body into a more natural rested state of being. Regular meditators witness an improved quality of sleep.

 ## Improves focus and concentration
Meditation has shown in research studies to increase focus and concentration, and enhances problem solving abilities.

 ## Can help reduce pain
Daily meditation encourages the body to move from the inflammatory response linked with chronic stress into the relaxed response. It's a useful aid in pain management and muscle tension recovery.

 ## Can help reduce depression
Daily meditation has been shown to be a helful aid in reducing depression and other mental health issues when taught effectively.

 ## Improves heart health
Regular meditation practice can be a helpful aid in reducing heart disease and stroke, and useful at lowering symptoms of high blood pressure.

Meditation has been used for centuries to cultivate a sense of inner calm, clarity, and connection. It offers numerous benefits for women by addressing your unique challenges and experiences. It's a valuable tool for women to enhance your health and well-being.

Techniques for Mindfulness Meditation

Mindfulness meditation focuses on developing awareness and acceptance of the present moment by recognizing and accepting thoughts, feelings, and sensations without judgment or evaluation. It helps restore balance to an overactive mind and body by remaining in the present moment when thoughts arise and allowing them to fall away naturally over time. Your thoughts can shape your reality for good or bad. So, feed the good thoughts! Feeding bad thoughts breeds negativity, stagnation, and keeps you from reaching your heart's desires. To be full of peace, love, and harmony, maintain positive thoughts. This doesn't mean you should live in fantasyland and avoid reality, it means to nourish the goodness around you. Overcome negative thoughts with positive energy to resist negative thoughts and self-talk that keep you captive.

The most common takeaway from mindfulness meditation is the deep calm and peace in that can last the rest of the day, week, or month. The main component of mindfulness meditation is to pay attention to whatever you are doing now and to resist negativity to feel calmer, more relaxed, and in control of your thoughts and emotions.

Guided audio or video recordings can help you advance in a group setting or at home. I personally prefer to meditate alone with some fantastic apps that have really helped me along my journey. The apps below are incredibly helpful:

- InsightTimer (my favorite)
- Moonly
- Calm
- IAm
- Buddhify

These apps have guided mindfulness meditations that can be performed at any time. There are also some fantastic guided meditation videos on YouTube as well.

I find it best to practice after waking up, before bedtime, when I'm feeling stressed, or when I have negative thoughts and emotions that impact my day.

There are several techniques to help you improve your practice.

MINDFULNESS EXERCISES

1

MINDFUL BREATHING

Focus on your breath, count your breaths, and be aware of your breath going in and out.

GRATITUDE PRACTICE

Take a few moments to think of something that you are grateful for and really let the feeling of gratitude sink in.

2

3

POSITIVE AFFIRMATIONS

Take time to repeat positive affirmations to yourself, such as "I am capable of achieving my goals" or "I am strong and capable."

MEDITATION

Take time to sit in stillness and focus on your breath or repeat a mantra to yourself or repeat your sacred feminine qualities.

4

5

BODY SCAN

Focus your attention on different parts of your body and notice the sensations as you move through each one.

WALKING MEDITATION

Begin walking normally, preferably in nature, while paying attention to your feet on the ground and breathing as you go about your chosen path. Stay fully present and aware of everything happening around you, to not take anything for granted and ensure your focus remains intact for the duration of the meditation

6

It's also important to note that mindfulness meditation is not an overnight solution. It is a practice, not a perfect. Just like yoga, it is a practice unique to you.

Mindfulness meditation is not a new concept. Many ancient traditions used this practice to address day-to-day needs, as well as helping to cope with difficult or painful situations. Mindfulness meditation helps you make more informed choices to help you become more aware of and take control of your thoughts and actions, to reduce stress which impacts everyone in some way throughout life.

Cultivating a Daily Meditation Practice

Daily meditation practice can have profound benefits for women to be less reactive and respond to events more positively. Those who practice meditation are better able to connect with others, and to achieve their goals more effectively. When I incorporated consistent, daily meditation practice, my world began to change for the better.

1. Make it part of your daily routine. Try to wake up and meditate for five minutes before beginning your day. You can even do this in bed. It's also possible to meditate on the bus, train, or in the workplace during breaktimes. Use headphones for guided meditations to help you get into the mindset.

2. Practice in groups if you enjoy group settings. This allows you to meet other people who also want to develop a meditation practice, as it helps you to be accountable and motivated.

3. Practice meditation independently. Some people like to meditate in the quiet of their home, but others prefer to do it in front of a waterfall, next to a campfire, overlooking the ocean or lake, or under the stars. I personally prefer to meditate independently in a beautiful space in my home free of clutter and distraction.

4. Develop a sacred playlist. When practicing meditation, be mindful of your music choice, to keep it soothing and not distracting. Select music to help you anchor you in the present moment.

The Sacred Playlist, Rise Sister Rise playlist, or the Divine Goddess Mix playlist on Spotify have all been instrumental for me during my practice. I listen to them while meditating, journaling and reflecting. The Calm app and the Moonly app also have sound healing clips and music to listen to while practicing meditation.

Just remember that cultivating a meditation practice can take time. To truly see results, I have found that staying consistent helps the most.

It's easy to get distracted during meditation and you might feel you aren't doing it correctly, but don't get discouraged. There's no right or wrong way. Again, it's a practice, not a perfect.

Once you've developed the habit of meditating, it will become much easier to do over time. For those interested in a more formal or structured meditation practice, you can take classes with a certified teacher. Teachers will guide you through each step of the practice. There's nothing wrong with getting some help along the way if it makes your meditation experience more effective.

Journal Prompt:

Set aside a few moments to jot down your intentions for starting or deepening your meditation practice. What are your reasons for wanting to meditate? What benefits do you hope to experience through this practice? What can you commit to? Take time to explore your motivations and expectations for this transformative journey.

7

Creating a Sanctuary in Your Home

" *I create a sacred sanctuary within my home, a space that nurtures my soul, replenishes my energy, and envelops me in tranquility.*

A home is much more than four walls and a roof. It is where you can be who you are to rest, rejuvenate, and prioritize health, an essential part of life. It's also where you can escape being bombarded outside distractions.

Finding a space in your home to nurture your soul and replenish energy is a vital part of this journey. Creating a sacred space can be deeply personal and empowering, so give it careful thought.

The Importance of Sacred Space

A sacred space is a designated physical space where you can retreat, reconnect with yourself, and cultivate a sense of well-being. The concept of a sacred space is significant, providing a nurturing empowering environment for self-reflection, self-care, and personal growth.

Creating a nurturing, healing space is one of the most caring things you can do for yourself and your family. If possible, take advantage of any opportunity to create this space in your home, even if it's simply a comfortable area where can dance every day, listen to music, or sit in nature.

Hopefully you have a space in your home where you can explore the limits of your soul. If you do not have a sacred space in your home, find a quiet place in nature, in a library, or share one with a friend.

If you live in chaos and clutter, you cannot find the calm for inner exploration and growth. Creating a sacred space can bring numerous benefits to your physical, emotional, and spiritual well-being. Here are some of the key benefits:

1.   **Stress Reduction:** A sacred space provides a haven to retreat from the outside world and its stressors. Spending time in this tranquil environment helps reduce cortisol levels and promote relaxation, leading to decreased stress and anxiety.

2.   **Enhanced Focus and Clarity:** A designated sacred space improves focus and concentration during meditation and reflection where the environment is free from distractions, allowing you to delve deeper into your mind and feelings.

3.   **Mindfulness and Presence:** A sacred space encourages you to be present in the moment. Being in this space can help you cultivate mindfulness and awareness, grounding you in the here and now.

4.   **Increased Self-Awareness:** Spending time alone in your sacred space provides an opportunity for self-reflection and introspection, which can lead to personal growth, better understanding of feelings, and a deeper connection with yourself.

5.   **Cultivation of Rituals and Routines:** Having a sacred space fosters the development of rituals and routines. Whether it's a morning meditation, journaling, or simply taking

a moment to breathe deeply, these practices bring structure and purpose to your life.

6.   **Emotional Healing:** A sacred space serves as a sanctuary for emotional healing offering a safe nurturing environment to process and release emotions, find solace, and gain a sense of peace.

7.   **Spiritual Connection:** For those on a spiritual journey, a sacred space is a place for connecting with higher powers, divine presence, or a deeper sense of spirituality. It provides a space for prayer, contemplation, and accessing inner wisdom.

8.   **Boosted Creativity:** A designated sacred space enhances creativity. It's a space free from judgment, allowing ideas to flow freely and enabling creative expression.

9.   **Physical Well-Being:** A well-designed sacred space incorporates elements that contribute to physical well-being, such as comfortable seating, soft lighting, and fresh air. Spending time in such an environment can lead to improved relaxation and overall health.

10.   **Empowerment and Intention Setting:** Your sacred space can be a place to set intentions and goals for your

life. It becomes a space to focus your energy and manifest your desires.

Remember that sacred space is highly personal, and its benefits may vary from person to person. The most crucial aspect is that it resonates with you and provides a space that nourishes your mind, body, and spirit in a meaningful and fulfilling way.

If you share a home with others who don't quite understand the importance of having a sacred space, here are some steps to help you create and maintain a sacred space despite external challenges:

1.   **Clarify Your Intentions:** Take time to understand why you want to create a sacred space and what it means to you. Knowing your intentions provides a strong sense of purpose and motivation.

2.   **Choose a Private Corner:** If you can't dedicate an entire room, find a corner in your home to make your own. It could be a small area with a comfortable chair, a cushion, or a large floor pillow. Ensure that it's a space where you are comfortable and relaxed.

3.   **Keep it Simple:** You don't need extravagant decorations or expensive items to create a sacred space. Use simple meaningful objects that resonate with you. This could

be a few candles, crystals, plants, a meaningful picture, or a favorite piece of art.

4.   **Set Boundaries:** Communicate the importance of your sacred space to others and ask for their support. Let them know that this space is essential for your well-being and you appreciate their respect for it.

5.   **Time it Right:** Choose a time to create your sacred space when you know you'll have uninterrupted time. when you know you won't be disturbed.

6.   **Use Headphones or Music:** If you need to meditate in a busy or noisy environment, consider using headphones with calming music or nature sounds to help you focus and create a sense of privacy.

7.   **Create a Portable Space:** If you're unable to have a permanent sacred space, consider creating a portable one. You can use a small box or bag to hold your meaningful items, and when you need your sacred space, unpack and set it up anywhere you feel comfortable.

8.   **Practice Mindfulness:** Embrace the concept of mindfulness and bring your awareness to the present moment, regardless of external circumstances. Immerse yourself in the sacredness of your space, even if it's temporary or not physically separate from the rest of your surroundings.

9. **Connect with Like-Minded People:** Seek support from like-minded individuals, in person or through online communities who understand the importance of sacred spaces and self-care practices. Sharing your experiences with others can be empowering and validating.

10. **Trust Your Inner Guidance:** Remember that the most significant aspect of a sacred space is the intention and energy you bring to it. Trust your inner intuition as you create and nurture this space, knowing it is significant for your personal growth and well-being.

Creating a sacred space is a journey of self-discovery and empowerment. Trust yourself and know that honoring your need for this space, you nurture your inner self and foster a deeper connection to your own spirituality and well-being.

Designing Your Sanctuary

Creating sacred space begins with allowing yourself the time and energy to do so. Pay attention to images that inspire peace or creativity. A sanctuary can be simple and functional by choosing colors that match your personality and the overall feel of your space.

What colors are you attracted to? What images evoke a positive emotional reaction? For example, if you're an artist, are you drawn to bold colors or serene images that give you a sense of calm? If you're more of a minimalist, you may lean toward minimalistic designs that encourage concentration and self-reflection.

Infusing Your Sanctuary with Positive Energy

A sanctuary is meant to be a place to relax, nurture your mind, and rejuvenate. This can only happen if the space is infused with positive energy to allow you to meditate with nature. Adding items filled with positive energy to your sanctuary will make it more inviting and "magical." The space will feel sacred space where you can beat peace with yourself and your surroundings.

Positive energy comes from natural things like sunlight, plants, water, and spiritual practices. Foster positive energy in your sanctuary with the following ideas.

1. Choose colors that inspire you or match your personality. If your sanctuary is meant for self-reflection and tranquility, use colors that inspire creativity, well-being, and peace of mind to create a calming experience. Choose neutral or earthy shades of green, gray, brown, and beige for a calming mental effect.

2. Decorate your sanctuary by decorating with nature as much as possible to be surrounded by what makes your space unique and inspiring. Add natural materials like plants, stones, dried leaves, and wood chips for a rustic touch to create an atmosphere of seclusion and peace.

3. Layer images or keep it simple. Decorate your sanctuary with images that inspire you or reflect your personality and how you want it to be portrayed to make it feel personal and unique. Images and nature are a great way to inject a sense of seclusion and tranquility into your sanctuary.

4. Use a crystal as your sanctuary lamp. The crystals can be any that uplifts the mind and body. Some examples of crystals that work well include clear quartz, blue topaz, amethyst, or tiger's eye.

The stone color will depend on your preference but choose one that is heart-shaped or possesses specific colors like green, pink, or violet. These stones promote a sense of calmness and peace. Himalayan salt lamps are great too, because they can improve air quality, enhance your mood, and help you sleep.

5. Use candles as a source of positive energy. Candles create positive energy by burning to foster an atmosphere of tranquility and relaxation. Light candles in the sanctuary to breathe in the aroma. Choose candles with high quality waxes and organic oils.

6. Use incense as a form of positive energy. It is best used sparingly, since too much will have the opposite effect and become too overwhelming after prolonged use. To burn incense in your sanctuary, light one stick at a time and allow it to burn for just a few minutes.

7. Use an essential oil as your sanctuary fragrance to bring positive energy into your sanctuary. Essential oils have been used for centuries. Use pure essential oils from plants such as lavender, lemongrass, sage or geranium, since they promote a sense of serenity and calmness. There are also many essential oil blends you can create as well. Use the scents you're drawn to that provide a sense of peace and tranquility.

8. Use music as a source of positive energy. Choosing relaxing music to help you center, to start your day, or calm yourself after a long day at work. It can also be used as an alternative form of meditation to induce self-hypnosis or take time for the mind to rest. There are apps for your phone, such as the Calm app, that have a variety of background soundscapes and music for you to play in your sanctuary. This fills the room with positive energy promoting tranquility, calmness, and a relaxing experience.

9. Clear the clutter. This is crucial when creating a sanctuary as it fosters a harmonious and tranquil space, allowing room for positive energy flow. When a space is cluttered it doesn't give room for the new. Getting rid of the old creates a vacuum for new intentions to be manifested.

These are just some ideas to create a sanctuary but take your time to find and create your space, for it is a deep part of the sacred self-care journey. Putting sincere thought into it will help yield the results you want to achieve.

Journal Prompt:

Imagine and describe your ideal sanctuary, a place where you feel safe, nurtured, and peaceful. What elements, sensations, and experiences do you want to incorporate into this sanctuary? How can you use it consistently to help you feel grounded and centered?

8

Crystals for Healing and Chakra Balance

"I harness the healing energy of crystals, embracing their power to restore balance and harmony within my mind, body, and spirit.

This may or may not be for everyone, but I have learned that crystals are not only a beautiful gift of the earth, they are also powerful. While scientific research on crystal healing is limited, ongoing studies in the field of vibrational medicine and alternative therapies find that they're a natural remedy that help with anything from healing to balancing energy.

Crystals represent balance and serenity. They are believed to hold memory or the essence of their environment. They are credited with many healing properties, from balancing the body, mind, and spirit to increasing self-esteem and emotional growth.

An Introduction to Crystal Healing

Crystal healing is an alternative practice using crystals and gemstones to promote balance, healing, and well-being. It is based on the belief that crystals possess specific energies and vibrations that interact with the body's energy systems to bring about positive changes. Cultures worldwide have used crystals throughout history to heal body, mind, and spirit.

Crystals have held significant cultural and historical importance throughout human civilization and can be incorporated into any spiritual practice. They can enhance whatever spiritual practice you currently participate in and don't take away from your love of God, Buddha or any other deity.

Here are a few examples of their historical significance:

1.   **In ancient civilizations** crystals were utilized for various purposes. For instance, ancient Egyptians believed that

crystals had protective healing properties. They used lapis lazuli, carnelian, and clear quartz in their jewelry, amulets, and burial rituals.

2.   **Traditional Chinese medicine (TCM)** has used crystals as an integral part of medicine for thousands of years. In TCM, crystals like jade, amethyst, and rose quartz are believed to promote balance, well-being, and vitality. They are often used in acupuncture, energy healing, and as massage tools.

3.   **Native American cultures:** Crystals hold spiritual and ceremonial significance in many Native American cultures. They are used in rituals, vision quests, and as healing tools. For example, the quartz crystal is considered a sacred stone by many Native American tribes. It is believed to amplify spiritual energy.

4.   **Ancient Greek and Roman civilizations:** Crystals were highly regarded in ancient Greek and Roman civilizations. For instance, the philosopher Aristotle believed that amber possessed healing properties, and Greek philosopher Theophrastus wrote about the properties of crystals and their potential medicinal uses.

5.   **Medieval and Renaissance periods:** During this time, crystals were sought for their perceived mystical and

healing qualities. Alchemists and occultists such as Paracelsus and Cornelius Agrippa attributed specific properties and powers to various crystals, incorporating them into their practices and writings.

6.   **Traditional healing systems:** Crystals have been utilized in various traditional healing systems worldwide. For example, Ayurveda, the ancient Indian system of medicine, incorporates crystals like amethyst, coral, and turquoise for balancing energy and promoting well-being.

It's important to note that while historical significance provides insights into cultural practices and beliefs, it doesn't serve as scientific evidence of crystal healing properties. The historical significance of crystals showcases the enduring fascination and appreciation of their beauty, symbolism, and potential metaphysical properties across diverse cultures throughout history.

Crystals are believed to work through several mechanisms. They may emit specific vibrations that resonate with certain aspects of the body's energy system, helping to rebalance or remove energetic blockages. They also act as amplifiers or conductors of energy, to enhance energy flow within the body. Additionally, crystals may have symbolic or psychological associations that influence an individual's mindset and emotional well-being.

Crystals for Balancing Chakras

Chakras are energy centers believed to exist within the subtle body according to certain spiritual and healing traditions, including Hinduism, Buddhism, and various New Age practices. The term "chakra" originates from Sanskrit, and it means "wheel" or "disk." Following is a brief overview of the traditional understanding of chakras.

1. **Seven main chakras:** The most commonly recognized system comprises seven main chakras aligned along the body's central energy channel, called the Sushumna. Each chakra is associated with specific physical, emotional, and spiritual qualities.

- **Root chakra (Muladhara):** Located at the base of the spine, it is associated with stability, grounding, and basic survival instincts.

- **Sacral chakra (Svadhishthana):** Located in the lower abdomen, it is associated with creativity, pleasure, and emotional well-being.

• **Solar Plexus chakra (Manipura):** Located in the upper abdomen, it is associated with personal power, self-esteem, and confidence.

• **Heart chakra (Anahata):** Located at the center of the chest, it is associated with love, compassion, and emotional balance.

• **Throat chakra (Vishuddha):** Located in the throat, it is associated with communication, self-expression, and truth.

• **Third Eye chakra (Ajna):** Located just between the eyebrows, it is associated with intuition, insight, and spiritual awareness.

• **Crown chakra (Sahasrara):** Located at the top of the head, it is associated with spiritual connection, higher consciousness, and enlightenment.

2.   **Energy flow:** The chakras are believed to be interconnected energy centers that allow the flow of vital life force energy, known as prana or chi, throughout the body. When the chakras are balanced and open, they are thought to support overall well-being and harmony.

3.   **Imbalances and healing:** It is believed that imbalances or blockages in the chakras can lead to physical,

mental, or spiritual disharmony. Various practices, such as meditation, energy healing, yoga, sound therapy, and specific visualizations are used to balance and activate the chakras, promoting healing and optimal energy flow.

How to Unblock a Chakra

You might explore unblocking or rebalancing your chakras through specific yoga poses, targeted breathing exercises, and meditation practices.

Diane Malaspina, PhD, a therapeutic yoga medicine specialist, shares she prefers to think of chakras as out of balance versus blocked. She explains, *"There can be a depletion of energy flow or too much energetic activity in a chakra, where each will manifest different outcomes."*

According to Malaspina, when a chakra is low in energy, you'll have difficulty expressing the qualities associated with that chakra. When a chakra is overactive, according to Malaspina, its qualities exert a dominant influence on the person's life, potentially leading to both physical and emotional effects.

She recommends the following to promote balance in a chakra by creating alignment in your physical body through the following.

- Yoga postures
- Breathing practices to encourage energy flow
- Meditation to restore clarity of mind

When the main seven chakras are open and balanced, energy can freely flow through your body and mind. When these energy centers are blocked, though, it leads to stagnation and contributes to a variety of physical and spiritual ailments. If you experience stiffness or recurring pain, read along to see if a chakra imbalance could be a potential cause and find out how chakra balancing might help.

If you're anything like me, after reading the following chart you may recognize that one or more chakra is imbalanced or blocked. This happens when one is blocked, and the other chakras begin to compensate for it and can become overactive or underactive. So, the best way to start balancing your chakras and work toward well-being is to start at the root and work your way up to the crown, one chakra at a time.

Which Chakra
is **BLOCKED?**

ROOT	**SACRAL**	**SOLAR PLEXUS**	**HEART**
Muladhara	*Svadhisthana*	*Manipura*	*Anahata*
Survival, Safety, Security, Grounding, Life Force	Sexuality, Relationships, Joy, Pleasure, Emotions, Creativity	Self-Esteem, Power, Ego, Strength, Transformation	Love, Empathy, Kindness, Compassion, Gratitude, Faith
Color: Red	**Color: Orange**	**Color: Yellow**	**Color: Green**
LAM	VAM	RAM	YAM

I AM	**I FEEL**	**I DO**	**I LOVE**
I am centered & grounded. I love being in my body. I am safe.	I embrace my sexuality & I honor my desires. I deserve to enjoy life.	I feel my power and I act with courage. My potential is unlimited	I love myself and others. I follow the voice of my heart.

Represents: Safety, security, stability and foundation

Represents: Creative, Passionate, Sensual energies

Represents: Self Esteem, Pleasure, Will Power and personal responsibility.

Represents: Peace, Self Love, Compassionate, Kind & Governs our Relationships

Unbalanced: Apathy, Fear, Laziness, Anxiety, Depression, Insecurity, Lack of Motivation, Weak Physical Health

Unbalanced: Addictive Behaviors, Expressiveness, Drama, Seeking Attention, Lack of Desire, Insecurity, Anxiety, Guilt

Unbalanced: Competitive, Angry, Aggressive, Low Self Esteem, Lack of Energy, Powerless, Egotistical, Manipulative.

Unbalanced: Needy, Helpless, Tired, Clingy, Exhausted, Afraid to Let Go

Blocked: Overly stressed about money, security and/or survival, ungrounded, flighty, generally fearful, feeling of not belonging anywhere, poor health

Blocked: Emotionally cold, Difficulty Changing, Difficulty experiencing Joy, Holds Back.

Blocked: Lack of Confidence, Difficulty manifesting desires. Lack of Self Esteem.

Blocked: Lack of Confidence, Difficulty manifesting desires, Lack of Self Esteem, Lonely, Lack of Purpose, Overly Attached.

Overactive: Overly practical, lacking dreams and imagination, Habitual, Tied down, Difficulty letting go

Overactive: Hyper Emotional, Overly Sexual, Overly focused on physical pleasure, guilt

Overactive: Misuse of power, Dominance, Over reliance on will, Shame.

Overactive: Unhealthy Relationships, Loving Too Much, Love Manifesting at a Low Vibration

Physical Symptoms: Problems with legs, feet, rectum, tailbone, and immune system

Physical Symptoms: Sensual and reproductive health issues, Urinary problems, kidney dysfunctions, Hip, pelvic and lower back pain.

Physical Symptoms: Digestive Problems, Chronic Fatigue, Pancreas and gallbladder issues

Physical Symptoms: Asthma, Upper Back and Shoulder Problems, Arm and wrist pain.

Issues with the male reproductive parts and prostate gland

Gemstones: Carnelian, Garnet, Gold Tiger's Eye, Stilbite, Orange Calcite, Moonstone, Amber, Golden Topaz

Gemstones: Citrine, Topaz, Heliodite, Fire Opal, Amber, Gold Tigers Eye, Pyrite, Sunstone, Aragonite

Gemstones: Rhodonite, Rose Quartz, Green Agate, Amazonite, Green Opal, Jade, Peridot, Aventurine, Chrysoprase

Degenerative arthritis, knee pain, sciatica, eating disorders and constipation

Gemstones: Red coral, Black Obsidian, Bloodstone, Tourmaline, Red Jasper, Red Tiger's Eye

THROAT
Vishuddha

Communication, Expression
Authenticity, Purification

Color: Light Blue

HAM

I SPEAK

I hear and speak the
truth. I have integrity, and
I live an authentic life.

Represents: Honesty and the
ability to speak and
communicate clearly.

Unbalanced: Fear of
Speaking, Shyness, Social
Anxiety, Lack of Trust,
Secretive, Critical, Gossipy,
Unauthentic

Blocked: Inability to
communicate ideas, Problems
with Self Expression
(Expression of own truth)
Problems with creativity.

Overactive: Uncontrolled, Low
Value, Inconsistent
Communication, Manipulative,
Deceitive of Self or Others.

Physical Symptoms: Thyroid
Issues, Sore Throat, Ear
infections, Neck and shoulder
Pain.

Gemstones: Turquoise, Black
Lace Agate, Aquamarine, Blue
Howlite, Kyanite, Amazonite,
Aqua Aura

THIRD EYE
Ajna

Intuition, Imagination,
Lucidity, Astral Projection

Color: Indigo

OM

I SEE

I am insightful and
intuitive. I see clearly,
and I think clearly

Represents: Intuition,
Clairvoyance, Foresight, and
driven by openness.

Unbalanced: Fearful,
Delusional, Full of Anxiety and
tension, Irrational, Illogical,
Psychic Disorders, Brain Fog.

Blocked: Lack of Imagination,
Lack of Vision, Lack of
Concentration, Blocked or
Clouded Intuition, Can't see
"big picture".

Overactive: Distorted Vision,
Delusional, Distorted
Imagination, Misuse of
intuition

Physical Symptoms:
Headaches, blurred vision,
and eye strain.

Gemstones: Sodalite, Lpais
Lazuli, Azurite, Sapphire,
Dumortierite, Emerald, Kuanite,
Calcite, Celestrel.

CROWN
Sahasrara

Consciousness, Unity,
Spirituality, Oneness

Color: Violet

OM

I KNOW

I am one with the Divine
I honor the Divine within
me and around me.

Represents: States of Higher
Conciousness and divine
connection

Unbalanced: Loneliness, Lack
of Purpose, Weak Faith,
Depression, Detatched from
Divine, Spiritual Disconnection.

Blocked: Ungrounded,
Impractical, Indecisive,
Difficulty with Finishing things,
No Common Sense,
Depressed, Alienated,
Confused.

Overactive: Cut off from
Spirituality, Plagued by sense
of Meaninglessness,
Delusional, Grandiose.

Physical Symptoms:
Coordination issues,
Chronic headaches and
migrains, Chronic fatigue
Amnesia, Hair loss
Pituitary gland malfunctions

Gemstones: Clear Quartz,
Moonstone, Howlite, Amethist,
Quartz, Labradorite, Sugilite,
Geode.

If you're uncertain about where to begin or wish to gain more insight into your chakras and their potential impact, consider seeking the guidance of a professional energy healer, such as a reiki practitioner, or consulting with a certified yoga instructor.

Incorporating Crystals Into Daily Life

Start small when incorporating crystals into your daily routine. Don't feel the need to go overboard with your first purchase; you can even start with just one crystal. Choose a crystal that resonates with you. Crystals have different meanings for different people, and your crystal will be most effective when you choose one tied to the areas you aim to develop and improve within yourself.

Be realistic about the benefits you will get from a crystal. Don't expect a crystal to perform miracles. Some of the perceived healing effects of crystals may be attributed to the placebo effect, where you can experience positive changes due to belief in their healing properties. However, I emphasize that the placebo effect itself can have powerful and valid impacts on well-being. Crystals can act as a symbol to help heal your body or mind but be realistic and don't use crystals alone without incorporating all the other areas of sacred self-care discussed in this book.

The following chart shows how different stones can be used for healing the different chakras.

Chakra Healing Stones Chart

Many people use crystals and stones as a method of healing. Below is a chart of two examples stones for each Chakra that can be used for healing. There are four for the heart Chakra since it has two colors related to it. Simply lying on your back and placing the stones on your body above the corresponding Chakra can cleanse negative energy, balance each Chakra, and release emotion.

Chakra	Stone	Image	Uses/Properties
Root	Red Tiger's Eye		Grounding, protection, physical vitality
	Garnet		Stimulate survival instinct, increase willpower and courage
Sacral	Carnelian		Physical desires, relationships
	Orange Calcite		Enhances creativity, brings positive energy to areas of will and sexuality
Solar Plexus	Citrine		Personal power, worldly success
	Topaz		Encourage self realization and confidence
Heart	Aventurine		Love, balance, healing
	Jade		Love, Healing, Money, Protection
	Rose Quartz		Balance between heaven and earth
	Kunzite		Love, Power, Good Luck, Healing
Throat	Sodalite		Ability to speak openly and lovingly
	Lapis		Verbal expression, clear communication
Third Eye	Amethyst (Dark)		Understanding and intuition
	Sugilite		Teaches and protects in matters of spiritual quests, love, and forgiveness
Crown	Clear Quartz		Spiritual connections
	Amethyst (Light)		Enhances spiritual awareness and spiritual wisdom

Keep your crystals in a safe place, in the open in a bowl or tray. When you're finished using a crystal, put it in a place to recharge for the next time you need it. Some healers recommend charging them under the full moon every month.

Crystals work best when used with other stones and healing methods, so don't abandon other methods to rush into crystals. Start by incorporating one or two crystals into your life and enjoy their beauty as symbols of your healing journey.

Remain open-minded when incorporating crystals. Working with them is a great way to practice mindfulness and intention setting. The act of consciously engaging with crystals and setting positive intentions can be a valuable aspect of personal growth and well-being, regardless of the physical properties of the crystals themselves.

It's important to note that while chakras have long-standing cultural and spiritual significance, their existence and effects are not scientifically proven. The understanding and interpretation of chakras may vary across different traditions and individuals. Some view chakras metaphorically as a means of understanding and exploring one's inner self, while others perceive them as tangible energetic centers.

Journal Prompt:

Reflect on physical, emotional, mental symptoms, or patterns you have noticed in your life that could indicate blocked chakras.

Consider each of the seven main chakras and their associated qualities. Are there specific areas where you feel stuck, lacking, or out of balance?

9

Self-Care Rituals for Women

" I prioritize self-care and honor my well-being by establishing nourishing rituals that replenish and rejuvenate my mind, body, and soul.

Self-care rituals provide dedicated time and space for women to replenish their energy, restore inner harmony, and cultivate a deeper connection with themselves. These rituals go beyond mere self-indulgence and foster a profound sense of self-love, self-compassion, and self-awareness. By engaging in regular self-care, you enhance your overall quality of life, improve relationships, and cultivate a positive and empowered sense of self.

The essence of self-care rituals lies in the intention behind them. These rituals are purposeful and serve as a means of self-nurturing and self-empowerment. They offer an opportunity to slow down, tune in, and prioritize one's own needs and desires in a world that often encourages women to prioritize the needs of others. Self-care rituals allow you to reconnect with your inner wisdom, honor your emotions, and practice self-compassion, all essential to maintain a healthy fulfilling life.

In a society that often values productivity and external achievements, it's essential to recognize that self-care isn't selfish but rather an act of self-preservation and self-love. By prioritizing self-care rituals, women can refuel their energy, and show up as their best selves in all areas of life. Whether carving out small pockets of time each day or dedicating special occasions for self-care, these rituals serve as a potent reminder that women's well-being matters, and they deserve to invest in their happiness and fulfilment.

Self-care rituals are more than something that looks good on a to-do list. They can be life-changing, primarily when they're rooted in the values of spirituality and self-love. When you practice self-care, you honor your unique value and beauty as a human being.

As you incorporate these rituals into your life, don't be surprised if they become a source of positive energy, inspiration, peace, love, and rejuvenation. We all have days when we feel depleted and run-down. Finding time to nourish your body and soul can be difficult when caught in the thick of stress and busyness.

Self-care rituals should be tailored to your individual needs and preferences. It's important to make self-care a regular part of your routine to maintain your overall health and well-being.

The Importance of Self-Care

Although we've discussed this before, I can't stress it enough. Self-care is often misunderstood as an act of self-indulgence. However, the primary aim of self-care is to enhance self-love and embrace the inherent value we all possess. You can more readily love and honestly care for others when you value yourself.

Sacred self-care rituals are vital because they offer women holistic care of their well-being in mind, body, spirit, and emotion. They are essential to maintaining healthy boundaries in life. As you honor your own needs, it's easier to honor the needs of others in your life as well. Self-respect and love consequently contribute to the strength of your relationships with others, which allows you to be more effective as parents, partners, friends, and workers.

When you don't take care of yourself in a balanced way, you may become irritable, stagnant, and impatient with those around you. Self-care is vital because it allows you to honor your health without being overly indulgent or unrealistic about your time and energy demands. I admit that when I'm overcommitting, staying busy and not taking at least 10 minutes out of my day devoted to nourishing my spirit, I can be short-tempered and irritable. I have made a commitment to myself to devote time to self-care exercises every day. I find that this practice really does promote wellness, and helps me nourish my mind, body, and spirit when I do so consistently.

Finding time and space to care for yourself can be challenging in a society where women are often encouraged to put others first. You may inadvertently exhaust yourself by being constantly available for others, but neglecting your needs is not a way of giving others what they want. Self-care is a way for women to take care of ourselves without sacrificing relationships or feeling resentful or angry toward those who place demands on us.

While there are many ways that self-care rituals have the potential to enhance your well-being and overall happiness, they can also provide a powerful connection with your inner wisdom and spiritual values. This is sacred!

Self-care rituals such as meditation and prayer can provide a space to quiet your mind, reflect deeply on your life, and develop a renewed sense of perspective about the critical elements of life. For women who are in a place of transition or change, these rituals may offer an opportunity for growth and healing.

It's important to remember that self-care is not an indulgent act but rather a form of self-love and self-respect. When women are willing to support themselves this way, it goes a long way toward restoring balance, reducing stress, and strengthening their relationships with others.

Establishing a Self-Care Routine

Establishing a routine to make self-care part of your everyday life is essential. A pattern can be as simple as taking a daily walk in nature that nurtures you on an energizing level. The following are some ideas for your self-care routine.

1. Set aside time for self-care. Finding a place to be alone and not be distracted is essential. During this time, put your phone on airplane mode, close the door, and remove unnecessary things that may distract from your practices.

2. Create a space where you can relax. Whether in a room of your house, a separate area of the house or at a park or beach, clear out clutter so there are no unwanted materials that might become sources of stress. Clear out any decorations or items of sentimental value if they no longer serve as valuable reminders about who you are or what you value.

3. Make sure the space is comfortable. Make sure you can sit or lie comfortably. You may wish to change your clothes to feel more in touch with yourself and your body, or you might want to remove makeup so your skin can breathe.

4. Bring in the tools you need. If you will be meditating, bring necessary items (candles, incense holders, incense, etc.) and a timer if you intend to dedicate time specifically for meditation. If essential oils help keep you grounded or relaxed, bring them along.

5. Set intentions. Decide on the overall sense of your self-care session. Whether you want to relax, do yoga, meditate, or pray, sit or walk in nature, determine what you want to gain from the experience.

6. Begin with centering techniques. Sit quietly and focus on your breath as it moves in and out of your body. You can use counting breaths or other forms of meditation to help you get in touch with your body and clear your mind before the ritual begins.

7. Focus on self-awareness. As you care for yourself, ask what specifics need to be met during this period. Ask, "What do I need to feel relaxed, satisfied, or relieved?" Start with basic needs and work toward your higher-self goals (e.g., "I need to relax my mind so I can make better decisions, be more creative, and communicate my ideas.")

8. Set intentions for your higher-level goals. While you're taking care of your basic needs, you often set higher-level goals as well. For instance, if you want to create more time for self-care by scheduling appointments that take up part of your day, identify the times to help you meet those goals. You might set goals to read in the morning, take a walk, or go to the gym during your self-care time.

9. Address negative emotions. Many women experience negative emotions when caring for themselves; addressing them is essential. If you feel angry, sad, stressed, or resentful, remember that taking care of yourself is part of being a good parent, wife, sister, friend, and worker. Just as you can choose not to put yourself in positions where you're at risk for negative emotions, you can also decide whether to allow yourself to be angry or frustrated with yourself while you care for yourself. Just try your best not to be critical of yourself if you find you're neglecting your self-care routine. Just jump back in when you can and have grace and patience with yourself.

Self-Care Practices for Mind, Body, and Spirit

Self-care practices vary depending on your individual goals and needs, but several methods are almost universal in their ability to bring balance and healing to your life. You can use techniques to manage stress, reduce anxiety, and find peace of mind. Below are some self-care activities to aid in your development on a spiritual, emotional, physical, and intellectual level.

Skin care / Dental hygiene routine – Establish a daily skincare routine that includes daily cleansing, moisturizing, and protecting your skin from the sun, as well as daily dental brushing and flossing.

A skincare routine is important for several reasons that contribute to the health and well-being of your skin. Daily cleansing helps remove dirt, oil, and impurities that accumulate on the skin throughout the day. This prevents clogged pores, acne, and other skin issues. Moisturizing is essential for maintaining skin hydration. It helps prevent dryness, flakiness, and the development of fine lines. Well-hydrated skin looks and feels healthier and promotes a more youthful complexion.

Maintaining good oral health is also connected to overall well-being. Inadequate dental hygiene has been correlated with a heightened risk of several systemic conditions, including cardiovascular disease, diabetes, and respiratory infections. Dental hygiene is crucial for maintaining oral health, preventing dental issues, gut issues, and promoting overall well-being. Consistent proper care, including brushing twice daily, and flossing once a day along with regular dental check-ups and cleanings, is crucial for achieving and sustaining optimal oral hygiene. This helps control the growth of harmful bacteria in the mouth, which in turn can prevent the entry of potentially harmful microbes into the digestive system.

Poor dental hygiene could lead to periodontal disease, causing inflammation and potential infection in the gums. Chronic inflammation in the mouth has been linked to systemic inflammation, which may contribute to conditions such as inflammatory bowel disease (IBD) in the gut.

Meditate – Meditation helps you find peace of mind and clarity of thought. Meditation is a form of self-care that can significantly benefit the mind and body. You may want gentle meditation, like guided imagery or simple breathing techniques. Meditating first thing in the morning every day for 10 minutes right after waking up is incredibly powerful.

Studies have proven that when you wake up, the brain is in a state similar to hypnosis. Listening to guided meditations that help boost energy, express love and gratitude, relax, work with emotions, address family and relationship issues, make decisions and many other types of guided meditations are all sacred ways to show self-love.

Self-reflect and journal your thoughts – Some people journal to understand their thoughts and feelings better. Journals can be valuable tools for women who want to learn more about what they're doing well and where they might need to change behavior.

I personally LOVE the Dear Universe journals by Sara Prout. They have helped me commit to journal daily, be more present with myself, be more grateful in general, and notice the things in my life that are positive.

Exercise – As we covered in previous chapters, physical exercise is key for physical and emotional health, as it helps keep your body healthy and provides outlets for stress. Moderate exercise isn't just good for the body, it can also be very beneficial for the soul by helping to clear your mind and provide a sense of accomplishment after you've accomplished a good workout.

Nurture your relationships – Although it may be tempting to avoid friends and family for extended periods of time, it's vital to nurture relationships with those who are important to you. Going out for coffee or lunch, going on a walk together, calling a friend and inviting them over regularly, sending cards or notes of encouragement, and attending social events can all help you feel more connected with others and inspire you.

Do something creative – Doing something creative is a way to help you clear your mind and gain a sense of accomplishment. Creating art, writing, reading, cooking, dancing, playing an instrument, crafting, and gardening are all great ways to express yourself and reduce stress.

Connect with nature – Nature is another way to connect with the universe. Walking outside to connect with nature is a form of self-care that helps many people find greater purpose in life. Many enjoy getting out in the morning while it's still cool to spend time by a lake, park, or beach to take in your surroundings. Nature has a calming effect and reminds you you're not alone but part of something much larger than yourself.

Take classes – Whether it's a formal academic class, a recreational workshop, or an online course, the act of learning can be a valuable enjoyable component of a self-care routine. It allows you to invest time in yourself, prioritize personal development, and contribute to your overall well-being.

Attend retreats – Retreats can be very beneficial for those who want to dig a little deeper to connect more with your soul and develop to your full potential. I recently attended my first solo retreat (without a friend to hold my hand) to the Yoga of Awakening retreat with Sean Corne and I can't tell you how transformative it was for me. She has a beautiful way of viewing the world with empathy, love and acceptance and I couldn't help but adopt her philosophies into my own life. Not only did I meet some amazing women at the retreat that I'm still in contact with today, I connected with a deeper part of my soul and released long-held emotions I was holding onto for decades.

Join a support group – This can be a proactive empowering form of self-care. It offers a sense of community, understanding, and resources to navigate challenges, foster emotional well-being and personal development. Support groups contribute to breaking down the stigma associated with certain issues by creating an open accepting environment. This helps them feel more comfortable seeking help and sharing their stories. Check your local area for an organization that can connect you with other women.

Take relaxing baths – Relax in a bath with Epsom salts, essential oils, or bath bombs to unwind and soothe your muscles. Turn the lights down, light candles, and play healing music to help you relax and melt into the moment.

Read – Set aside time to read books that interest you. Reading is both relaxing and mentally stimulating. Not only that but it's a great way to gain new knowledge and insight. None of us have all the answers and have more to learn in order to grow.

Get quality sleep – Give priority to sleep by setting up a consistent sleep schedule and cultivating a comfortable sleep environment.

Use aromatherapy – Explore the benefits of aromatherapy with clean essential oils to create a soothing atmosphere in your home.

Schedule time alone – Alone time gives you time and space to recharge and focus on self-care without distractions.

Limit screen time – Reduce the amount of time spent on electronic devices and social media to prevent digital overwhelm.

Set boundaries – Learn to say no and establish healthy boundaries to protect your well-being.

Seek therapy or counseling – Counseling provides a safe confidential space to express your thoughts, feelings, and concerns. A trained counselor can offer emotional support, empathy, and offer a safe space for healing from past trauma or challenging life events. Counseling can also aid in self-discovery and self-awareness. It helps you understand your thoughts, behaviors, and emotions, which can be crucial aspects of personal growth.

Massage and Reiki – Massage therapy can be an excellent source of self-care. Some massage therapists even offer reiki sessions to clients as a great way to relieve anxiety and promote relaxation. When you get a massage, remember it's not just about the physical work the therapist provides, the messages and the energy they send are therapeutic. A good reiki massage therapist will communicate with you during your massage and assist you in reaching your deeper mind, body, and soul goals.

Yoga – Yoga is another form of meditation that helps you stay connected to your body, mind, and spirit as you move through poses designed to help strengthen your body and relax muscle tension or pain. As discussed in Chapter 5, there are several types of yoga, each with a goal.

Although any of these self-care rituals can be undertaken at any time, as we mentioned in chapter 2, having an awareness around the seasons is helpful.

I consistently remind myself to take Rebecca Campbell's advice in her book, *Rise Sister Rise*, to develop a relationship with the changing seasons around me, to *"… notice the hope and inspiration of spring, the celebration, rising and outward connection of summer, the falling away and letting go of fall, and the replenishment, clarity, rest, surrender, and potency of winter. "*

This is a work in progress. Think about the seasons—fall, winter, spring, and summer. Rate the seasons from your most to least favorite. What is it about the seasons that make you feel invigorated or want to hibernate? What gifts of self-care do the seasons have that your body needs and wants? What can you do to honor them?

Journal Prompt:

Describe the self-care rituals you currently engage in. Reflect on activities that bring you joy, relaxation, and rejuvenation.

Write down just a SINGLE thing you can start doing tomorrow to commence a new daily ritual of self-care. That could mean waking up 10-15 minutes earlier to incorporate meditation, journaling, yoga stretches, clearing clutter or whatever you need to help keep you centered and grounded. Write about the benefits you experience from these rituals and how they contribute to your overall well-being.

10

Cultivating Positive Relationships

❝ *I attract and cultivate positive relationships in my life, surrounding myself with loving, supportive individuals who uplift and inspire me on my journey.*

Relationships are integral to well-being; they are one of life's most rewarding wells of happiness, providing a forum for sharing and experiencing various viewpoints, activities, affection, and love. Each of you contribute to relationships with other people with your own strengths and perspectives. A relationship is like a dance, an art you participate in to create something new, more wonderful than you could have done alone.

The value that relationships play in your life should not be underestimated. Relationships are the soil from which health grows; they fuel and nourish who you are as an individual and offer support and love. They make it easier to do the work of living, returning love when needed, or understanding someone else's perspective. Relationships provide comfort during hard times and celebrate triumphs. Positive relationships are essential for wholeness. They help generate the positive loving energy that fuels you.

The Importance of Supportive Relationships

Health suffers when we experience trauma or abuse. It's simply not possible to truly grow and heal in an unsupportive or toxic relationship.

If you're in an abusive relationship, it's crucial to prioritize your safety and well-being. Leaving an abusive relationship can be difficult, but there are steps you can take to protect yourself and seek help. Reach out for support by confiding in a friend or family member about your situation.

Contact a local domestic violence hotline or shelter for guidance and support. They can provide information on resources available in your area. Develop a safety plan to prepare for future incidents. This may involve having a bag packed with essentials, a list of emergency contacts, and a safe place to go.

Remember that leaving an abusive relationship is not easy, and it may take time to resolve your situation. It's important to prioritize your safety and seek professional help and support throughout the process. You are not alone, and there are resources available to help you escape an abusive situation and rebuild your life.

The more supportive, comfortable, and familiar a relationship is (and the stronger it is), the easier it is to overcome disagreements or setbacks. That's why healthy relationships are such an essential part of growth and self-care.

Trust is the willingness of two people to expose themselves emotionally by putting self-interest aside and honoring the other person's interests. In intimate relationships, the desire to share details about yourself makes you vulnerable to others and often brings joy and acceptance.

Sadly, the world contains people whose idea of relationships is based on the need to control or manipulate others. Still, in a healthy relationship (one marked by mutual trust and respect), both perspectives are fostered. This can be a rich source of support for each person striving for balance. So often, you (or others you're in relationships with) tend to try to control everything. Throughout history, when individuals or groups are driven to control and dominate, the consequences can be detrimental and lead to various forms of conflict, oppression, and suffering.

Holding onto outcomes without room for fluidity, compassion and understanding is a surefire way to crack under the pressure. The more rigid you are (or others around us) the more likely it is for someone to fall to pieces.

It's important to clarify that recognizing your lack of control doesn't mean you should become passive or indifferent. It means acknowledging the limits of your control while taking responsible constructive action within those limits. Ultimately, understanding that you cannot control everything allows you to lead a more balanced, emotionally healthy life, with greater resilience and the ability to adapt to life's unpredictability. The image below is a great reminder of what we can and cannot control.

What you Cannot Control

✗ What happens
✗ Others actions
✗ Others opinions
✗ The Weather

What you Can Control

★ My Perspective
★ How I respond
★ Being authentic
★ Self Care

Some of you may struggle with supporting relationships because you've had experiences in families or society that led you to keep your true feelings, needs, and thoughts to yourself. Many of you have been taught that speaking up is a bad thing and that you're wrong to feel the way you do, that you're "too sensitive" or you're shut down when you speak your truth. Many of you have learned to keep your honest thoughts and feelings a secret.

When you don't trust that your real needs and experiences will be heard and accepted, you can become disconnected from your wisdom because it feels dangerous to share ourselves. I know what it feels like to not feel safe to share my hopes, dreams and fears. It led me to do some very hurtful things to my partner and my shadow side surfaced in a big way. This was my third big awakening that shook me so hard I could no longer avoid listening to my soul.

To build relationships that support your health and well-being, you must learn to trust the power of your thoughts and feelings. This requires recognizing that there is no objective standard of "goodness" or "rightness", except what you define for yourself. You know your truth and trust the facts inside and out to guide yourself to healthy relationships.

The best support for your own health is the kind of support that comes from inside. You must learn to trust yourself and acknowledge that everyone's truth is as valid as your own. When you do this, you can love without judgment, appreciate others for who they are, and draw on your values to help make decisions for yourself. This way of being in relationships feeds into your ability to be whole and well in all areas of life and avoid self-sabotaging behaviors.

If you're lucky, you have people who love you for who you are and support your growth. This kind of love is an honest legitimate act of generosity that doesn't require you to give anything up or alter who you are in order to keep it.

When relationships help you feel good about yourself, they can be an excellent source of life support. You must believe that you deserve the best and know how to ask for help so you give yourself the support you need to feel whole and well again. When you set healthy expectations, supportive relationships empower you to move forward with optimism and courage.

Through the outward expression of values, you can enjoy and be part of supportive relationships, which remind you of what you value, what we are accepted for, who we are, and reinforces the belief that you have found worthwhile people in your life willing to give you room to grow and evolve ourselves. This helps you value yourself by accepting and loving others and giving everyone the space to be who they are.

Having support from people outside romantic relationships can also make it easier to feel fulfilled and bounce back from hard times. Bell Hooks, in her book, *All About Love*, beautifully describes how important friendships are and that devaluing them is a disservice to your well-being. She contends that, *"We often take friendships for granted even when the interactions are fulfilling. You tend to place them in a secondary position, especially in relation to romantic relationships."*

She goes on to observe that, *"This devaluation of your friendships creates an emptiness you may not see when you are devoting ALL your attention to a chosen romantic love, or giving all your attention to a chosen loved one. Committed love relationships are far more likely to become codependent when you cut off all ties with friends to give these bonds you consider primary your exclusive attention."*

Relationships are a part of who you are and continue to form in new ways, creating a network of influences that alter your perspectives and choices over time. They show you what is essential while enriching emotional connections. The truer and healthier romantic loves are, the less compelled you feel to diminish or cut connections with friends in an attempt to reinforce your bond with your romantic companion.

Establishing Boundaries and Communicating Needs

It is essential to realize that healthy relationships are not about controlling or manipulating each other but about making sure each party feels safe and respected in an open, honest environment.

Healthy boundaries in relationships allow the true expression of truth. I'll be honest that I did not know how to do that without either suppressing my feelings and needs or lashing out in rebellious ways.

I was raised to believe that a romantic relationship was superior above all else. Most women and men born in the 50s and earlier were socialized to believe that marriages or committed relationships should be prioritized over all other relationships. I found myself in a controlling, abusive five-year relationship in my first romantic relationship in my late teens and early 20s. I thought it was a sign of commitment and an expression of love to endure unkindness and cruelty, to forgive and forget.

For years after ending this unhealthy relationship, I chose to run in the opposite direction of this mindset, but in turn closed my heart and put up a wall that was nearly impossible to penetrate. I found myself wanting to love and share my most vulnerable self but kept my partners at a distance. I was scared to be open, fearing I wasn't safe to do so. My world came crashing down after it all came to a head in my current marriage. I realized I was suppressing my feelings, forgoing my needs, and allowing my husband to speak to me in a way that at times was disrespectful, hurtful, and cruel. I acted out and in retaliation and subconsciously made a decision that hurt my husband very deeply.

Looking back, I realize that our lack of understanding about the art of love put our relationship in jeopardy right from the beginning. Throughout the almost 18 years we've been together, we were preoccupied with reenacting familiar childhood dynamics, influenced by misconceptions about what constitutes a loving relationship. As a result, we failed to recognize the personal changes we needed to make to truly love another person.

I have learned that we must allow ourselves to have feelings and thoughts that may differ from someone else's. That means trusting that well-being is not dependent on everyone agreeing with everything we do or say, but that we are heard whether we agree or not. We can honor ourselves by setting healthy boundaries with others while being open to what they have to offer in return.

Tips on how to establish boundaries and communicate needs:

1. Learn to say NO and mean it! When you learn to say NO, you become more assertive. Sometimes saying no is the nicest thing you can do for yourself and others. Overcommitting and agreeing to do things you don't want to do, not only leads you astray from honoring your own needs and desires, but it often even disappoints others you care about. When you're too available, you can become overwhelmed and exhausted by the unnecessary demands of others. Saying NO is one way of setting boundaries in relationships, which helps others to respect your perspective and offers the ability to be who you are to express what you think and feel.

Develop your style of asserting yourself by learning how to practice saying no in different situations. Practice saying NO when your partner or friend asks you to do something that isn't in your best interest.

2. Communicate how you feel, and don't try to fix the other person's feelings. You're on your path of spiritual growth, and if you ask for what you need, it is up to others to decide whether they can fulfill that need or not. Everyone is entitled to their own feelings and sometimes you will disagree with how someone perceives a particular situation. However, acknowledging how they feel and listening compassionately is the ultimate sign of respect.

People have different needs. You may want to talk about something, but the other person may feel triggered, tired, or stressed at the moment, making it ineffective to have a discussion about something that may be upsetting. Asking to set aside some time later when one or both of you have some time to cool off and even putting it on the calendar can be effective. It's important to respect another person's boundaries and communicate your needs in a way that respects your feelings and abilities.

When speaking, be confident yet gentle in your delivery. Try not to be forceful or convince someone what you believe is right for them; that is coercion, which will lead to manipulation if there isn't healthy give-and-take in the relationship. Sometimes in heated disagreements, pause the conversation so both people can cool off and return to the conversation later. Set a time frame so one party doesn't feel dismissed and put off.

One of my favorite tools for couples is a book by Nancy Dreyfus, *Talk to Me Like I'm Someone You Love*. It's an incredibly helpful resource to help communicate with loved ones more effectively. I can't recommend it enough. It has helped my husband and I understand each other during disagreements. In Dreyfus' book, there are over 100 flash cards with written statements to help convey what you yearn to express to loved ones yet struggle to articulate due to lack of effective words or proper emotional tone. We looked through the book together and found statements we could relate to, which really gave us insight into each other's perspective.

3. Strive for mutual autonomy. Being able to respect each other's boundaries means being independent of each other without having to ask permission for every fundamental decision you make. You have to set limits for yourself and earn the right to question each other.

If you always ask permission, it gives other people too much control over your life and can feel you're constantly being judged or controlled. When this happens, you don't feel safe to act and not safe enough to express yourself honestly because you fear hurting someone else's feelings by standing up for yourself.

4. Practice active listening. Active listening is a practice that allows you to hear what the other person is saying without interrupting and to keep your physical and mental space while you're communicating. You can also take active steps to show support, such as giving a hug or reassuring a loved one you're listening empathetically. Active listening helps you get to know the other person better by making both of you feel heard and understood. This makes for greater clarity in expressing needs and desires.

5. Be genuine with yourself. It's impossible to express yourself honestly if you can't be yourself, and it's impossible to give or receive true love if you don't trust the other person's genuineness.

You must be good at communicating your needs because giving and receiving requires willingness to take a risk while understanding that it may not work out the way you want. But being genuine makes you more open and capable of truly loving another.

6. Set your own consequences. Recognize that setting boundaries and communicating needs means that consequences flow from actions. Before acting on something upsetting or frustrating, consider how your action will affect you. For example, if someone cuts you off on the freeway and you decide to speed up and slam on your brakes in retaliation, think about what that can cause. Ask yourself if it's really worth it. Having a sense of self-control makes a difference in how others react and respond to you.

7. Reassess and adjust daily. Be willing to reassess and adjust boundaries when circumstances change. Sometimes you have to reset your boundaries to be free to let things go rather than holding onto the past, which can cause stress and anxiety.

This is especially important in relationships with people going through a change or a growth process at the same time we are. You want what's best for them without holding them back from progressing while they're adjusting to a new situation. Holding boundaries can be challenging, so here are some phrases you can use to communicate with your loved ones.

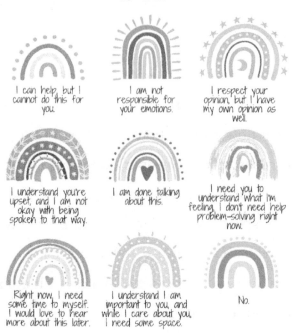

Boundaries sound like...

I can help, but I cannot do this for you.

I am not responsible for your emotions.

I respect your opinion, but I have my own opinion as well.

I understand you're upset, and I am not okay with being spoken to that way.

I am done talking about this.

I need you to understand what I'm feeling. I don't need help problem-solving right now.

Right now, I need some time to myself. I would love to hear more about this later.

I understand I am important to you, and while I care about you, I need some space.

No.

Building a Community of Empowerment

The list below helps create a supportive inclusive network of people who uplift, inspire, and encourage each other to reach their fullest potential. This fosters a sense of connection, collaboration, and shared growth among community members focusing on empowerment and mutual support.

Community building is an integral aspect of a healthy spiritual life. Being a part of an empowered community opens you to feeling empowered. This helps you feel less alone while sharing the growth and experience through relationships with fellow community members. The following are ways to build communities of empowerment.

1. Be willing to share experiences and perspectives. By sharing experiences and perspectives, you might better understand what others are going through, which can help everyone feel more supported and less alone.

Not everyone will share your knowledge or perspective, but sharing them in a kind, neutral way gives others greater insight into your feelings and who you are. Being open to sharing what you're going through with people who may not understand outwardly, you can create relationships that make others feel safe enough to practice their own vulnerability.

2. Be willing to listen without judgment. Listening is a skill that takes practice outside social interaction because it's difficult for most people to truly listen without judgment. For a community to work, it must have members who listen without judgment or agenda. This isn't easy because you're human and prone to put things and behaviors into little boxes. It helps to remember, however, that you've all had experiences that shaped you into the unique, one-of-a-kind being you are. Understanding that there's a lot of gray area in the world and that many things aren't black and white is something you should remind yourself of every day.

3. Be willing to help others. Nature helps you realize that we are all connected. We feed from each other's energy and share in each other's struggles. To protect yourself from being overwhelmed by the demands of others, you must be willing to set boundaries, but this doesn't mean you can't help others regardless. When someone is struggling, it doesn't necessarily mean they are a burden to you or want your time and energy so severely that they make unreasonable demands, like a child who hasn't learned how to respectfully ask for what they want or need. By helping others, you feel good about what you contribute to the world, and that you are not alone.

4. Be willing to share meaningful experiences. By sharing meaningful experiences, you're more likely to bring more meaning to life and share in the growth and understanding of others. The more of yourself and your stories you share with community members, the more connected they feel to you. This connection brings people together in relationships, resulting in a positive sense of empowerment rather than simply letting someone else take care of problems.

5. Be open to vulnerability. To truly connect with others, allow yourself to be vulnerable with them. Being vulnerable is sharing your experiences with others and being prepared to be seen by them. When you're in balance, you're more likely to give of yourself openly in an honest, non-manipulative way.

6. Be selective but open to feedback. Loved ones and community members should be respected enough to share thoughts and feelings openly and be valued enough to give and receive honest feedback. Suppose a community is not open to honest feedback. In that case, boundaries may be crossed, and others may feel unsafe within the community because their innermost secrets might be exposed without consent. Without honesty in a community, people won't know how they're genuinely perceived by other members, which could result in a relational conflict where none should exist. Oversharing sometimes can create conflict when trust is lacking. So use your intuition and be selective with whom you share you innermost thoughts, feelings and experiences.

Journal Prompt:

Reflect on relationships in your life that bring you joy and positivity. Can you be open, genuine, and safe to be yourself in significant relationships? What are the qualities and actions that contribute to its positivity or lack thereof?

11

Integrating Spirituality and Personal Growth

" *I connect with my spirituality, trusting my intuition and aligning with my higher purpose.*

Spirituality and personal growth have always been intertwined. One of the deepest ways to grow is to incorporate spirituality into your life. Today people often focus on the physical and tend to look outward for things to fulfill within. In today's society we are taught to place value on money, material things, recognition, success, and comfort. All those things are nice to have, of course, but oftentimes in comfort we tend to take things for granted.

Instead, you can ask what part of your soul is attracted only to comfort and pleasure? Does this allow you to evolve continuously? Your soul can grow from wisdom, experience, compassion, and love, as well as through challenging times.

A different perspective might be to see that discomfort teaches important lessons. It might offer deep opportunities to evolve and grow and to be grateful for times of comfort. You can know that both discomfort and comfort are temporary, and there are lessons in both to help you raise your consciousness.

When you truly grasp this understanding, it can lead to an awakening, a deep understanding and revelation of a higher wisdom. Real magic occurs when you recognize and embrace your connection to all other living beings. Be in awe of life, nature, the intelligence of the universe, the power of the sun, moon, earth, and water.

This understanding transforms your perspectives, attitudes, and behaviors by fostering more compassionate, harmonious, and sustainable ways of living. For most of my life, I've been disconnected from spirituality. As a child, I attended church with my mom and enjoyed the relationships built in the youth group, but other than that I didn't feel deeply connected to the beliefs of the church.

Don't get me wrong; I found many of the teachings to be valuable but the Christian Nazarene church I attended believed that dancing detracted from spiritual growth and would break down proper moral inhibitions and reserve. What? Um, that's a big NO from me.

Dancing is a form of expression, of art, of feeling free, and brings me joy. How could this be? How could the teachings of love, forgiveness, patience, and acceptance also say it's wrong to express yourself through dance? That you must stay within the lines and not truly express oneself? To teach acceptance, but also reject people attracted to the same sex. Isn't that a form of oppression? In my eyes it is, especially since my dear, sweet, loving uncle was gay and rejected by my grandfather. I couldn't reconcile the dichotomy.

I personally found the organized church to be threatening and fear-based. What I heard was, "do as you are told or be punished by God and live in hell for eternity". I really struggled with this mindset and felt a huge disconnect from organized religion. However, I have also felt disconnected from myself and for most of my life searched for contentment through material things — money, status, success, physical appearance, and sex.

However, in the depths of my darkness over the past year, I have connected with something greater. A divine force of limitless possibility and unconditional love, and a deep respect for a higher power.

We have many names for the divine forces. Whether you call this the almighty power God, Source, the Divine, Alah, Yahweh, Buddha, the Force, Goddess, Great Mother, Mother Earth, the Universe, or another higher source that resonates with you, the infinite energy behind it all is the same. Whichever you connect with or don't connect with, you need to understand that both light and dark beings live here.

There are powers of good and evil at play in this world. You can begin to meet people and experience understanding that the divine is at work in everyone and everything.

Exploring Your Spiritual Path

Exploring your spiritual path is a personal journey of self-discovery, introspection, and growth in connection with your spiritual beliefs, values, and practices. It involves seeking a deeper understanding of your spirituality, exploring different belief systems, and finding meaning, purpose, and fulfilment in your spiritual life. You can find fulfilment in your path if that path is a true reflection of your beliefs.

Regardless of who you choose as your deity, your relation to what you regard as sacred, absolute, spiritual, and divine is worthy of deep internal respect. Conventional religion can feel restrictive for some, as it did for me but choosing to live in a spiritual way is no more than an ideal that can be used to guide you into a deeper understanding of yourself and connecting to the world around you.

If you're looking to find a spiritual path, it can be helpful to seek out others who are like-minded and non-denominational in belief, meaning they don't restrict their opinions to a single sect or church. Don't be afraid to pursue your spiritual path, even if it differs from your peers or family. While you may sometimes feel alone on the journey, remember that many others have also taken similar journeys of self-discovery before you. They learned how to develop a routine to honor their spiritual self.

Use your inner strength to find the courage to pursue a more meaningful life. There may be obstacles along the way, as there always are, but by facing them head-on with open eyes, you can better experience peace within yourself.

Sometimes you may come to a fork when choosing a spiritual path. If possible, it's always wise to take a step back and reflect upon the way you genuinely feel is right for you. Don't be afraid to change direction if something doesn't feel right.

Remember, it is YOUR spiritual journey, and no one has the right to tell you which way to go or how far down the path you should travel. Once you've chosen your spiritual path, be sure to keep your eyes and heart open, but always beware of those who might be motivated to take advantage of the weak. Your spiritual path should align with your values and lead you to growth and enlightenment, not to be manipulated, taken advantage of, controlled, or coerced.

As with anything in life, there will be times when your personal beliefs do not mesh with those of others around you. Don't let those differences prevent you from connecting with others around you. It's better to make friends with those who think differently than to stay locked in your bubble. While it may seem like others are trying to block your path, tune out those fears and remember that your course belongs to you. While it may be tempting to turn back, never give up on yourself.

Embarking on a spiritual path is a profound transformative significant journey in your life. It's a personal exploration of the deeper aspects of your being, a quest for meaning, connection, and self-discovery. By delving into your spirituality, you can tap into a wellspring of wisdom, inner strength, and empowerment that can profoundly impact your life. It goes beyond religious affiliation or adherence to specific traditions, a profoundly personal and individual journey. It invites you to connect with your inner self, your intuition, and the divine forces guiding and inspiring you.

Exploring the spiritual path can be a transformative experience impacting ALL aspects of life. It can influence relationships, self-care practices, decision-making processes, and well-being. It offers a space for you to tap into your intuition, embrace your authentic self, and cultivate a deep sense of inner peace and harmony. Your spiritual journey provides the opportunity to connect with like-minded individuals, forming communities of support, understanding, and shared growth. These communities foster a sense of sisterhood, where women can celebrate each other's unique journeys, learn from one another, and provide mutual encouragement. While there is no set definition of "spiritual," different individuals will define the term differently and have diverse understandings of what it means to be spiritual. A woman's beliefs, values, and practices represent her spiritual journey. It is whatever you deem it to be and may change over time.

Exploring your spirituality does not just impact yourself, but also impacts those around you. As you explore your inner self, you learn more about the world around you with love and compassion.

You come to understand we are all connected, to respect earth and allow letting go of a sense of separation and judgement based on the color your skin is, your sex, your sexual preferences, where you were born, the religion you believe in, and material possessions you may or may not have.

By cultivating a sense of inner peace, you can also better cope with the challenges and struggles inevitable in life. You may find it easier to let go of past hurts, move on, and create new bonds. The sense of self-worth and empowerment you gain fosters a sense of gratitude for the richness and diversity of life.

This appreciation for the interconnected web of existence can lead to a more positive and grateful outlook on life, leading you to a renewed sense of purpose. It helps you communicate with kindness and show empathy, enhancing your ability to relate to different perspectives and promoting compassion.

Practices for Spiritual Development

Embarking on a spiritual path allows you to connect with your intuition and inner knowing. Rather than relying solely on intellect, which can cloud your understanding of the world around you, you can draw on a more profound sense of wisdom from within.

Walking the spiritual path can deepen your understanding of yourself and others, making it easier to process emotions and make better decisions in all facets of life. It can help you identify what you genuinely value and be more discerning in your choices, allowing you to choose respectful, loving, supportive, and nurturing partners.

It is influential to seek out mentors when embarking on this journey. While it's possible to find mentors from within your community, finding mentors who are not directly connected to your personal life is also beneficial. Outside mentors can provide unbiased advice and guidance that may be more objective than what women receive internally.

The following are practices for spiritual development for women:

1. Meditation. Meditation can calm the mind and connect you to your inner self to draw upon your spiritual power. You'll see the most benefits by doing so for a few minutes every single day. Sometimes that may not be possible, so try to meditate at least two or three times a week. Sit quietly, get comfortable and still your mind, breathing in through your nose and out through your mouth. If thoughts come into your head, let them come; it's natural to have thoughts. Use your thoughts to clean, rinse, and clear the mind to help you find your purpose and align with your goals. Allow them to come and pass.

2. Prayer. Create prayer rituals that include meditation and focused thought about what you wish to embrace spiritually. This includes ways of expressing gratitude for what you already have in your life. You can also release dark thoughts by writing them down and burning the paper, allowing yourself to eliminate them.

3. Affirmations. You can repeat positive affirmations to yourself out loud or silently in your head and gradually bring them to your conscious mind. Positively affirming the things, you wish to embrace helps bring you into the present moment, where you can more fully manifest your desires.

4. Journaling. Recording thoughts in a journal can be a powerful tool to connect your spirituality by providing a dedicated space for reflection, exploration, and expression of your inner thoughts and experiences. This is an effective way to self-reflect, set intentions, process challenges, record dreams and insights, track personal growth, practice gratitude, and gain clarity of beliefs.

5. Art. Women can express spirituality through any art form, freely exploring the inner self and releasing what is pent up inside. Art can also enable women to connect with a larger community with similar interests and values.

6. Prayer groups and sacred circles. Throughout history, women have formed prayer groups and sacred circles to come together regularly to pray, releasing their spiritual concerns into the universe while acknowledging the strength and support already within them.

7. Sacred sites and pilgrimages. Some women find that visiting sacred sites helps them tap into a sense of spirituality they may not be able to find at home or on the job. These sites can have spiritual power, serving as focal points where the divine and the human intermingle. They can also create sacred sites by visiting certain parts of nature where they feel at one with the world around them—perhaps a waterfall, ocean, lake, or trail.

8. Service. Women have the power to improve the world around them, making spiritual growth an integral part of their work. Given the opportunity, companies with high ethical standards are more successful in the long run than those not striving for these ideals. We can choose to work for companies or volunteer in communities that help feed people in need, provide healthcare and education, and combat injustice and oppression worldwide. Women who understand how deeply interconnected they are to the surrounding universe use service to connect with it on a deeper level. We can also increase our happiness by serving others, finding meaning in work, and feeling at one with the universe.

9. Ritual. Women can perform rituals to honor their spirituality, incorporating various forms of art, beauty, music, and dance into these celebrations. They may invite others to join them in these celebrations, which help them feel supported on their spiritual journeys. Women also incorporate rituals into daily life to mark important moments, such as changing seasons and holidays.

Aligning Your Life with Your Values

Values help prioritize what is most important in life that guides decisions. They help bring a sense of meaning to life and unity with others by connecting one person to another through a sense of shared values.

Understanding and aligning your life with your values is an empowering process that allows you to live authentically, make choices aligned with your beliefs, and create a sense of fulfilment and purpose. Values are the guiding principles that reflect what is truly most important to you and help navigate life's decisions and challenges.

To align your life with your values, it's essential to identify and clarify them. This requires introspection and self-reflection. Ask yourself what matters most, what brings you joy and fulfilment, and what principles you want to prioritize. Examples of values include honesty, compassion, integrity, non-violence, growth, freedom, love, creativity, moderation, and balance, among many others.

Once you have a clear understanding of what your values are, you can begin to align your actions, choices, and behaviors accordingly. Some strategies to help you align your life with your values are as follows.

1. Find like-minded folks. Find people who share the same values as you and get together with them regularly, or at least once a month to connect with other like-minded individuals. This helps you find people on the same wavelength and vibration, especially when you get together in groups where there is less risk of being alone and feeling uncomfortable or vulnerable.

2. Take steps toward living your values. Think about the behaviors that reflect your values and take steps to incorporate them into your life. For example, if compassion is one of your core values, commit to offering it to others. Or if you want to live a life of integrity, avoid doing something against your values.

3. Confront your values. Once you understand what you believe in, resist the urge to rationalize or justify. Rather than going through the motions to appear as if you live by your values, do it by example without argument or defense. Focus on behaviors that connect with your values. Living by example instead of pushing your beliefs on others is the best way to stay true to your values and earn respect for your beliefs. No one wants to be preached to. Living authentically by example is the only way to truly live in alignment with your values.

Should friends or loved ones want to know more about your journey, they have opened the door for you to share. Other than that, resist the urge to preach. That is exactly why I decided to write this book. Instead of shouting from the mountaintop to anyone that would listen, I decided to put it all on pen and paper to those interested in establishing a practice of sacred self-care.

4. Create moments of reflection. Whether alone or with friends, reflecting on your values can help bring them into focus and allow you to question them, challenge them, and see if they align with your life.

5. Make choices in line with your values. When you need to make a decision whether big or small, think about how the choice reflects your values and make it based on that. Rather than allowing external influences to sway you in another direction, follow what you know is true for you as a woman who knows what she values.

6. Take responsibility for your actions. Once you choose to align with a value, take responsibility for it rather than blaming others or making excuses for your behavior. Blaming others avoids owning up to what you did, making no changes moving forward, while making excuses wastes time and serves no purpose other than justifying the wrong choice.

7. Practice gratitude regularly to help you remember your values, reflect on critical principles, and bring a sense of fulfilment into your life. Gratitude enables you to take stock of everything in your life that matters and provides a sense of interconnectedness with everyone around you. Allow yourself to be moved by beauty in the world.

When you just can't seem to find something to be grateful for, go out in nature, look closely at the intricate details of a flower, a feather, or a shell, and look up at the sky. There is always more to see above: the clouds, the stars and moon, birds flying, trees swaying, and so much more.

Women can learn to live a life of authenticity, interconnectedness, and fulfilment by embracing their spirituality and all it offers. As we become more spiritually aware, we grow in positive ways both individually and collectively.

Journal Entry: Do I obsessively focus on physical outward things for fulfillment? What aspects of myself have I developed beyond the physical? Take time to consider the idea of body, soul, and spirit. Sense the possibility of connecting to divine beings and higher truths. Reflect on how to intentionally integrate spiritual awareness into your daily life to foster ongoing personal development.

12

The Power of Gratitude and Affirmations

" *I embrace the transformative power of gratitude and affirmations, cultivating a mindset of abundance and positivity that attracts blessings and manifests my deepest desires.*

Gratitude and affirmation are the two most important skills you can build to stay on track for healthy living. They are internally and externally powerful.

Affirmations represent thinking beyond feelings of how you want your life to be. Gratitude creates a positive energy field that draws what you desire into your life. Affirmations can be applied to anything you want to bring into your life. One of the most important things you can do is use statements that reflect health to nudge your thinking away from victimhood to empowerment.

The Science of Gratitude

Gratitude is, in essence, giving thanks for all the good things in your life. Research has shown that many benefits come from a grateful approach to life. People who practice gratitude have healthier hearts, improved immune systems, and better sleep. They are also more resilient and less materialistic.

I recently watched the documentary film, Heal by Kelly Noonan Gores. The film takes the viewer on a scientific spiritual journey to discover that changing one's perceptions, beliefs, and emotions the body can heal. I found it fascinating!

Gratitude isn't gratitude when you feel obligated or fake. It's an attitude of appreciation that comes from deep within your spirit and reaches out to touch everything around you. You don't just say thank you because people expect it of you; you do it because it makes your heart sing. Your heartfelt thankfulness adds a whole new dimension to life — a dimension of joy, lightness, and offering yourself as a beacon of hope to others. One way to focus on gratitude is to list everything in life you're grateful for as soon as you wake up in the morning, before checking emails, socials or text messages.

You can be grateful for your health, your home, your children, friends and family, the good you do, or the sunshine and the birds singing in the trees. This exercise will help you appreciate what's already around you to provide a concrete starting point for expressing gratitude to others. If things are really challenging and it's difficult to think of something to be grateful for, think about the little things, like having a comfortable bed to rest in, nutritious food to eat, a good cup of coffee, good health, quiet moments, or comforting music.

Gratitude makes you feel lighter and more accessible, bringing a sense of well-being that eases depression, fear, and anger. It's also a powerful healing agent. When you're in a state of gratitude, you clear out old blockages, limiting beliefs, and negative emotions, and usher in positive thoughts and a new way of being.

Developing a Gratitude Practice

Starting a gratitude practice not only helps you conquer negativity and depression, but it will also provide a sense of clarity and direction. It will help you stay focused on your goals, appreciate the opportunities that come your way, and help you make the most of each day.

Gratitude works because it changes your focus from negative to positive. If you're in a place of giving thanks for all the good in your life, you are naturally inclined to be positive toward others and to see challenges as growth opportunities.

Gratitude is more than just saying thank you; it is deep appreciation that makes you reach out with open arms to embrace what life has brought into your world. It's not a technique or a magic formula; it's a state of being you develop through your commitment to grateful thinking.

Like any practice, you must commit to practicing gratitude daily to see the benefits. It can be challenging; it takes work and persistence, but it's worth every effort you put into it. The following are ways to develop a gratitude practice.

1. **Give thanks first thing in the morning.** Before doing anything else, before checking your phone, think instead of at least three things you're grateful for. Science has proven that

how we wake up in the morning has a major impact on the entire day. On waking up, the brain is in a state similar to hypnosis, so starting your day right can make a powerful difference in your life. Be specific and include benefits like health, happiness, family, friends, love, nature, and spirituality.

2. Create a gratitude journal. Journaling can be a powerful way to honor gratitude. Create a place of expression and reflection where you can write your deepest feelings and thoughts. Journal each day at the same time, in the same place, with the same pen and paper.

3. Choose your challenges. Choose the most critical ones and think about what that challenge is trying to teach you. For example, if your challenge is that you live with chronic pain, think about what you're supposed to learn from it. Use it as fuel to propel elevating yourself and what you can offer to the world from your experience. Be thankful for your health and family, using that to offer kindness and help to others who may also live with illness or pain.

5. Be grateful for others. Be thankful for everyone you encounter—neighbors, the market clerk, or someone you recently met. Think about one positive thing that stands out about them and why. Show gratitude to others by smiling or giving a compliment.

6. Go outside. Nature is one of the best places to express gratitude. Take time to look into the sky or around your environment and be aware of the life surrounding you.

7. Take action. If there are things you want to see more of, give thanks for them, and act to make it happen. Select a daily power item, just one task to commit to for the day. For example, if you want to commit to yourself more, choose one thing to focus on right after waking up. Think of three things you're grateful for while listening to chakra-balancing or other relaxing music.

8. Smile. A smile is an outward expression of gratitude and happiness. When you smile at others and yourself, it radiates positive energy that brightens your mood and the surrounding environment.

Using Affirmations for Personal Growth

Affirmations are positive statements you say to yourself to change your beliefs and mood. Growing research indicates positive structural effects of affirmations on the brain. Engaging in positive affirmations introduces new concepts to the brain by creating and expanding neural pathways. It facilitates a shift from a mindset dominated by negative self-doubt to one characterized by positive confidence. Scientists have documented brain changes that occur when individuals opt for optimistic perspectives that actively construct and strengthen neural pathways. Science shows that we have nothing to lose and everything to gain simply by using positive affirmations on a daily basis.

This is not about reciting facts or stating the obvious; the purpose is to affirm an idea that gets you closer to your heart's desires by encouraging positive thinking to create a better future for yourself. I love the "I am" app, which allows you to choose areas you want to focus on. The app will send you daily affirmations as a reminder to engage them daily.

Affirmations can be a valuable tool for securing a positive mindset and building resilience. Combining affirmations with other positive habits, such as goal setting and self-care, can contribute to a more comprehensive approach to personal development and well-being. In a sense, affirmations are a form of prayer. They are a way of asking for what you want and giving thanks for what you already have.

The following are some guidelines on how to create affirmations.

Focus on one statement at a time: Create your affirmation or use the example affirmations below to give you some ideas. Write down everything within the scope of your pledge. For example, if you want more abundance in your life, include health, happiness, and material prosperity in the same statement. Don't try to write down too many affirmations at once; start with just one.

Be specific: Be very clear and precise in your request. Clearly specify your goals or the qualities you want to develop. Specific affirmations are more powerful and help focus on particular aspects of your life. Example: Instead of saying, "I am good at my job," say, "I am consistently improving my skills and excelling in my job."

Be positive: Choose positive empowering words. Frame your affirmations in a way that inspires confidence and optimism. Example: Instead of saying, "I will not fail," say, "I am confident in my ability to succeed."

Don't use negative words: Focus on what you want rather than what you want to avoid. Avoid the words **not** or **won't** in your affirmation, the universe doesn't hear them. Example: Instead of saying, "I am not afraid of challenges," say, "I embrace challenges as opportunities for growth."

Be realistic: Set the bar to be achievable; affirm that you can pay your bills this month instead of declaring that you will make a million dollars daily.

Use present tense: Phrase your affirmations in the present tense as if your desired outcome is already happening. This reinforces the belief that your goals are achievable now. Example: Instead of saying, "I will be happy," say, "I am choosing happiness in this moment."

Affirmations are just one of the many ways you can use positive thinking to change your life. However, be open to adjusting your affirmations as your goals evolve. As you make progress, your affirmations can evolve to reflect new aspirations.

Engaging in daily affirmations not only measurably enhances your resilience and stress management, but also yields positive effects on depression and anxiety. Consistent practice of affirmations contributes to the reduction of cortisol and adrenaline, and the detrimental stress hormones. As your stress response diminishes, there's a corresponding decrease in heart rate and blood pressure, mitigating the risk of stroke and heart attack. Individuals incorporating affirmations into their routine are also inclined to adopt healthier lifestyles, engaging in regular exercise, and maintaining a balanced diet.

When you create affirmations, focus on a single purpose, such as attracting more money, or improving your health. Speak to them out loud at least three times daily and then go into meditation to reach your subconscious mind. Vibrate each word to help it get deeper into your heart and soul. When you say an affirmation correctly, it has a magical power to attract everything within its scope.

There are some great apps you can install on your phone with affirmations. I really like the I Am app that gives daily positive affirmations to use. Here are some other great positive affirmation examples:

Self-Love and Self-Acceptance:

I am worthy of love and kindness.

I embrace my imperfections; they make me unique.

I am enough just as I am.

I radiate confidence, self-respect, and inner harmony.

My self-esteem is growing every day.

Health and Well-Being:

My body is healthy, and my mind is sharp.

I am grateful for the vitality and energy that flows through me.

I make choices that nourish and support my well-being.

Every day I am getting healthier and stronger.

I am at peace with my body and accept it as it is.

Success and Abundance:

I am a magnet for success and good fortune.

Opportunities are always coming my way.

I trust in my ability to create the life I desire.

Abundance flows to me effortlessly and generously.

I am open to receiving all the prosperity the universe has to offer.

Positive Mindset:

I choose joy and gratitude in every moment.

My thoughts are filled with positivity and my life is plentiful with prosperity.

I am in control of my thoughts, and I choose positivity.

Challenges are opportunities for growth and success.

I attract positive circumstances into my life.

Confidence and Empowerment:

I believe in my abilities and express my true self with ease.

I am confident, capable, and strong.

I am proud of my achievements and celebrate my successes.

My confidence is soaring, and I am unstoppable.

I trust myself to make the right decisions.

Relationships and Connection:

I attract positive loving relationships into my life.

I am surrounded by supportive uplifting people.

My heart is open. I attract healthy and loving relationships.

I am a magnet for kindness and compassion.

I am worthy of deep, meaningful connections.

Positivity in Challenges:

I am resilient, strong, and can overcome any challenge.

Challenges are opportunities for growth, and I am thriving.

I trust the process of life and embrace its challenges.

I face difficulties with courage and optimism.

I am in control of my thoughts, and I choose peace.

Feel free to personalize these affirmations or customize your own based on your specific goals and areas of focus. The key is to make them resonate with you personally and to repeat them consistently for the best impact.

Journal Prompt:

Reflect on aspects of your life for which you are grateful and areas where you'd like to cultivate a more positive mindset.

What is ONE thing you can do every single day to get your mind into a state of positivity? What three things you are grateful for today?

Consider how expressing gratitude and affirmations contribute to your overall well-being. Write down your thoughts and intentions.

Embracing Your
Wholeness

" *I embody inner strength, cultivating resilience and embracing the power within me.*

Throughout this book we've discussed what we need to cultivate our wholeness so now we can work to begin embracing and maintaining it. Remember embracing wholeness is about love and compassion for your body, mind, and spirit. It's a commitment to yourself to be a valued priority in your life. You can begin to love your body even when it doesn't show off its best features. Make peace with the chaos of life, honor yourself, and create a space of self-esteem where you feel great about who you are.

As a woman, you are beautiful and strong; you can love and be loved. I'm so happy you're reading this book! You have a wonderful spirit full of life. As you embrace your wholeness in this process, you can feel empowered and in charge of your life. You can find joy in the little things that make your heart sing. Your mind and body will become peaceful and experience a sense of wholeness from living within self-love.

When you recognize that you're divinely perfect and beautiful on every level, it goes a long way in creating the life you want.

Reflecting on Your Journey

Look back at times in your life that were uncomfortable or distressing and think about what that experience taught you. It turns out that behind every painful experience, trauma, or wound, there is often a gift. That gift is a way to get you to listen to what that experience is trying to teach you and find a way to overcome it.

The path of becoming whole, complete, wholehearted, comfortable with yourself, and loving all your characteristics and abilities is a journey of ups, downs, and everything in between. There will be dark times. That is a certainty. Become masterful at keeping your light on so you know how to navigate the dark when it comes. Find what lights you up and do more of it. When your fire is lit, you're more able to light the torch of others.

If you find yourself in the dark or feeling dull, numb, disconnected, angry or hurt, stop, and take time to really listen to what your soul is trying to tell you.

Maintaining Balance and Harmony

Keep your mind open; your body can heal itself if you're prepared for it to do so. Your mind can learn positive ways of thinking if you allow it to, and once you do, you'll begin to see things change in your life for the better.

Life can be unbearably stressful and unfulfilling at times. Sometimes it's difficult to keep your balance when life tries to knock you down. There will be things that knock the breath out of you, making it increasingly difficult to keep your balance. Stress is a natural part of life but finding ways to manage that stress and commit to showing yourself love and caring more during these times is crucial. When the human body is under stress, we're in a constant fight, flight, or freeze mode, and cortisol and adrenaline can stay elevated, which can trigger ailments.

There are three main stressors in life:

1.   **Physical stress** - accidents, injuries, falls, trauma.

2.   **Chemical stress** - bacterial infections, viruses, heavy metal exposure, hangovers, hormone imbalances, pesticide exposure, and blood sugar levels.

3.   **Emotional stress** - family tragedies, loss, financial, and emotional abuse.

Figuring out ways to manage stress is critical to maintaining a state of equilibrium, homeostasis, and balance. That's why it's incredibly important to work with doctors that treat the WHOLE person and surround yourself with people that inspire hope and strength instead of fear. What you think, believe, and how we feel WILL have an impact on your health.

We must practice self-love consistently, not only when we're exposed to stress. Maintaining balance in your life is important, so when things are out of control emotionally or physically, you'll know where to turn.

Just remember to take care of yourself first and the human mind can create anything you allow it to, negative or positive. It's a choice you make from day to day or moment to moment that ultimately determines the course of your life.

Live your life as a spark of brightly shining light after being hidden behind years of dreary darkness. This is the time to shine your light for the world to see.

Continuing Your Path to Healing

Your cheerleaders are people that love you. Those people that are threatened by your growth are not your people. Remember that not everyone can handle the success of others, so if someone feels threatened by your success, keep them at a distance. It's easy to let others discourage you or let a seemingly insignificant comment derail your progress. So, share your dreams and hopes only with those that you can trust with your heart and guard your peace as if your life depended on it.

If you're going through a hard time, always seek a trusted confidant who has overcome similar situations. Surround yourself with trusted confidants if you have them. Getting the perspectives of others can be very valuable and can help to keep you on your path to healing.

When you surround yourself with positive people and their positive energy, it will positively impact your growth journey.

We all have different views on life, and there will be times when we disagree with others. However, we have a choice to express ourselves and differing opinions with grace. We can agree to disagree, and that is perfectly okay. Stay true to yourself and leave others to express themselves as they wish, as long as it is done in a healthy way without causing harm. We can only change our own thoughts, our own actions, and our own emotions. We do not have control over the actions and emotions of others.

In the past, I have been guilty of becoming triggered when someone else shared a differing viewpoint, especially when it was positioned as something I should also believe, think, or do. I HATE being told what to do or forced into doing something I don't agree with. I also have to remind myself that not everyone agrees with me either, and not to push my own viewpoints on others. All we can do is kindly share our viewpoints with others who are open to sharing and receiving other ideas, views, and opinions, but not to push them to accept if they don't want to.

This is a form of emotional healing and emotional intelligence, especially after the world shut down in 2020 due to Covid. Humans tend to have negative responses when times are hard, scary, and uncertain. Among them are anxiety, fear, stress, panic, avoidance, catastrophizing, control-seeking behavior, addictions, agitation, and social withdrawal, to name a few. The ability to navigate uncertainty is a skill that can be developed over time through experience and self-awareness.

Emotional healing is a gradual process, and different individuals may experience it in unique ways. However, there are some common signs that suggest progress in emotional healing. These signs may vary depending on the nature and extent of the emotional wounds. How can you tell when healing is happening? Here are some good signs to pay attention to. Pat yourself on the back when you see them in yourself.

Signs That You Are
HEALING

Breaking
Old Patterns

Managing
Emotions

Forgiving
Yourself

Validating
Yourself

Accepting
Support

Setting &
Maintaning
Boundaries

Conclusion

The journey to an awakened life can feel challenging but is well worth the effort. Women who are first responders to their health and committed to wholeness will live more fulfilled, soul-led lives.

With consistent practice and time, you will witness that restoring balance and wholeness in all parts of your life will bring about positive changes for yourself and all those around you. The transformation can be profound, providing positive energetic energy in all areas of life. The art and beauty is that it can take you on a fantastic adventure within that you have likely never known before.

Accepting change can be uncomfortable, but it doesn't have to remain so forever. The more we become comfortable with change and flow, the more we're open to what lies on the other side. If you're not at ease with change, then it's in your best interest to seek the help of others, or a professional who can help guide you. But if you desire to make this journey, be prepared for initial discomfort and become aware of the need to adapt with the ups and downs of life.

You CAN evolve just like life evolves. Just like water, movement may be slow and gradual, but it makes a lasting impact.

Women, like water, have multi-faceted natures — the calm and the fierce human nature and the instinctive nature (conscious or unconscious), the civilized and the wild, the feminine and the masculine, the yin and the yang. The dualities of a woman's nature should work together, and as a result she is stronger. When both are in balance that's when magic happens. The female soul is more stable when there's a consistent ebb and flow. Even the healthiest psyche can lose its way. Remind yourself to live from the soul as opposed to the ego.

Th ego can hold us back; it tends to avoid learning. Remember that the real task is to repeatedly remind yourself to remain or return to a level of consciousness. Remind yourself of the following and repeat it like a mantra:

- I can sense and learn new ways of being.
- I am resilient and able to ride the storms when they come.

- I am patient and can learn to love deeply.

Repeat these mantras daily and ask yourself the following questions to remain conscious when feeling unbalanced or tangled between the ego and the soul, the dark and the light, or the too good girl and the wild woman:

- What do I need to give up to have more life?
- What should be disowned or eliminated to make room for continued growth?
- What am I afraid to give birth to now or in the future, and why?

A butterfly comes to mind. We don't know whether a caterpillar knows if it's dying, in pain, or sleeping while in its chrysalis. Does it know that in the darkness and struggle that it's being transformed? Upon awakening the caterpillar is rebirthed and emerges victoriously as a beautiful butterfly more capable and beautiful than it was before. With time, patience, and discomfort, it emerges from darkness into the warmth of the sun as a new living thing with wings to fly to greater heights with new beauty and power.

Just like you can't force a flower to open, it needs to be fed and nourished to blossom on its own. Just like a caterpillar's chrysalis can't be cut open when it seems to be struggling, it must go through the death and rebirth process in order to evolve into something more beautiful than it ever could have imagined.

Nourish your beautiful rose, let your butterfly go through its transformation, feed your inner goddess and what it needs to consistently remain in a state of your higher good.

How do we do this, you ask?

First, fuel your fire, burn with passion, with ideas, with desire and what you love. Your creative life (like a pot on a stove) needs a consistent fire underneath it. Don't forget to add fuel and to stir. The fire requires watching so the flame will not go out. Feed whatever nourishes your soul. Without the fire, your ideas and thoughts will remain unfulfilled and unnourished.

Tend to the environment you're in. Keep your mental & physical space clear of clutter, keep a clear space for your work and a clear head to complete your ideas and projects. This requires spending time each day for contemplation and reflection, a space that is your own, dedicated to your work with the materials, tools, elements, conversations, and freedom to do your soul work. Sometimes we neglect the importance of this space. It can become overgrown and be overtaken by the forest. Don't let the structure of the psyche become a lost ruin. Tend to your environment with consistent cyclical sweeping, and cleaning.

Your wildness, your fire, your intuitive knowing will thrive when you have a clear mental and physical space. Cleanse your thinking and ways of doing that no longer serve a purpose for your higher good.

Separate the ingredients in your pot and learn to make distinctions in judgment. When facing a dilemma or question, when the answers to solve it are unclear, come back to it later. The answer may lie deep in the subconscious, and there may be a good answer waiting in your dreams. Ask a question before sleep to receive an answer upon awakening. Separate and determine the difference between old ingredients that wreak havoc and new ones that nourish and stimulate the mind and soul. Distinguish between real love and mistaken love, from healing plant medicines and ones that can kill.

Clear the weeds and sort the ingredients. Some ingredients are meant to nourish the mind and some cause pain; others stimulate, and some terminate. Learn to differentiate thoughts from feelings to see and positively react to the negative shadows of your own mind or negative parts of people and events outside you.

I have found the Sightless Oracle website to be a useful resource for interpreting dreams; consider keeping a dream journal.

Keep a garden, either mental or real one. A garden teaches many lessons. What can happen to a garden can also happen to the soul. There can be too much heat, or too much water and vice versa, infestations, storms, weed invasions, dying off, healing, blossoming, bounty, and beauty. The cycles of life, death and rebirth are part of nature.

Keep a journal, recording what contributes to giving life. Take notes on what gives YOU life and what doesn't. What are you learning?

Intuition is a flame with power — keep it lit. Sometimes we fear intuitive power and may be tempted to throw it away thinking it's easier, safer, or convenient. It creates work to understand the inward and outward negative forces and imbalances that plague us. It creates an effort to gather the strength to fix what we now see that we may have avoided. The light that allows you to see also illuminates miracles, and the profound beauty in the world brings us into new consciousness.

As a clever fox or a wolf follows its instinctual nature, you dear goddess, can skillfully learn to find and keep your intuitive flame lit and hold your head high, with your crown shining brightly. For doing so is a form of self-love and it is sacred.

Whatever you do, don't hide your magic! Keep your flame lit and remember to light the torches of your sisters along the way.

So, I leave you with the lyrics of a beautiful song by Amber Lily. Her heartfelt songs shed light in my life during a dark time. Come back to this book or listen to her songs, when you need a reminder to brighten the light in you.

Wild by Amber Lily

We're separated by the hateful things they taught us to believe.
But naturally we're breaking free; it's a patient meditation,
Cultivating strength in me.
But I know my heart just wants to sing.

To howl at the moon, sing to the stars.
Howl at the moon, sing to the stars;
Remember who we are.

Who do you think you are?
What have we come to be?
Oh, the light that shines in you is the same flame that burns in me
So go on live your truth said you inspire me.
I wanna see you dance,
I wanna hear you sing, yeah.

Howl at the moon sing to the stars.
Howl at the moon sing to the stars.
Remember who we are.

I remember we are wild,
Still living in astound.
The earth, the wind, the water and the fire

When all else fades away, they remain,
Reminding us we've always been.
And we're still wild
We've always been.
And we're still wild (we're still wild).
We've always been (we've always been, and we're remembering),
And we're still wild (we're still wild).
We've always been (we've always been, and we're remembering),
And we're still wild (we're still wild)
We've always been.

Sitting at the edge I call to the ocean in me:
Come and teach me
Of your mystery.
I am open,
I am listening, I am listening.

Bow to the earth and greet the sun.
Bow to the earth and greet the sun.
Bless the land we walk upon.
Yeah.

Howl at the moon sing to the stars.
Howl at the moon sing to the stars.
Remember who we are.

Acknowledgments

My deep appreciation and gratitude go out to the many talented people whose support was essential in the creation of this book. To Sophie Howard for giving me the tools and vision to help me make this idea of writing a book into a reality. To Jan Mayden for giving me the structure to begin this beautiful project. To Barbara Lauger and Pavel Stanishev for your help with editing and to Lea Androic for her beautiful cover artwork that inspired me to begin this work in the first place. I'm grateful to Deborah C. Blanc for assembling the beautiful cover design.

I want to thank my parents for their unconditional love and for instilling within me a deep connection to nature. Thank you, Mom, for being my biggest cheerleader. I am eternally grateful for your never-ending love and support.

To Kendra Puryear for introducing me to the world of healing and understanding modern spirituality. To my childhood friend Michelle Mullholland for being a sounding board and for your loving advice.

Finally, thank you to my amazing husband for his love, support, and encouragement, providing me with the space to grow while demonstrating a willingness to evolve alongside me.

Made in the USA
Las Vegas, NV
16 January 2024

84482482R00144